Slay Your Day

How to get more done, become ultra-productive, and unlock your full potential!

Sandi Glandt

Copyright © 2020 by Sandi Glandt

All rights reserved. No part of this publication may be reproduced, distributed, or transmitted in any form or by any means, including photocopying, recording, or other electronic or mechanical methods, without the prior written permission of the author, except in the case of brief quotations embodied in critical reviews and certain other noncommercial uses permitted by copyright law. For permission requests, write to the author at the address below.

sandra.visnov@gmail.com

Although the author and publisher have made every effort to ensure that the information in this book was correct at press time, the author and publisher do not assume and hereby disclaim any liability to any party for any loss, damage, or disruption caused by errors or omissions, whether such errors or omissions result from negligence, accident, or any other cause.

ISBN: 978-1-951503-17-8 (Ebook)
ISBN: 978-1-951503-16-1 (Paperback)

Published by Authorsunite.com

Dedication

To my Bubbie. The ultimate Pioneer woman of her time. You are my greatest inspiration to show up every day as the best wife, mother, businesswoman, family member, and friend I can be. You have paved the way and shown me everything is possible! I look up to you and respect you for all you are, everything you've accomplished, and everything you stand for. If I turn out to be half the woman you are, I will thank my lucky stars! Thank you for blazing the trail and making the "balancing act" of doing "IT ALL" possible for all the success-minded, driven, and ambitious women today.

To my Mom and Dad. Mom, if not for you I wouldn't be half the woman I am today. You are a FORCE! You've taught me to be strong and brave, not to take NO for an answer, and convinced me I can do anything I put my mind to. It's because of your grit and fire I turned out to be the strong, independent woman I am proud to be today. Dad, you taught me early on what being an entrepreneur meant and looked like. You have a heart of gold and always wear it on your sleeve. Thank you for showing me at an early age what hard work, commitment, and building your own dreams look like!

To my loving and supportive husband, Jarrod. Thank you for supporting me every step of the way. From my crazy ideas, postpartum moments, brainstorming with me at night, and helping me turn my dreams into reality. There is no one else I would rather be on this amazing journey called life with than you. You are the calm to my crazy, a sounding board for my goals and aspirations, and you make me a better wife, mama, and woman! I'm so blessed to have you by my side. Thank you for your unwavering love and support.

To my Jakey boy. You are my greatest teacher! You are the little boy who came into my life and blessed me as a mommy. You've taught me so much about myself and about life. If not for you, I wouldn't have this burning desire and mission to help ambitious mamas (and women) all over the world to tap into their fullest potential. It's because of you I was able to see this in myself. Thank you for helping me change the world and make it a better place. You were born to move mountains, my baby! Because of you, I am able to live out my own mission and passion to be the best mama, wife, and businesswoman I can be. I am so proud of the little boy you are and the man you will be.

CONTENTS

Introduction 1

1 ~ Breakdowns Bring Breakthroughs 9

2 ~ Helping Success-Minded Women Be the
    Best Version of Themselves 19

3 ~ Trading Overwhelm for Purpose 27

4 ~ How Much Is Your Time Worth? 37

5 ~ Protect Your Time 47

6 ~ Know your NON-Negotiables 61

7 ~ The 3D System to Step into Success 71

8 ~ Organizing Home and Work 83

9 ~ Take Back Control 95

10 ~ Claiming Your Power as a Woman Who
     Wants to HAVE IT ALL 103

11 ~ Slay Your Day Today and Every Day 115

About the Author 123

Introduction

Hi! I'm Sandi and I am so glad you are on this journey with me! You may be here for many different reasons. Whether you want to get your life in order, become more productive, connect and have more intentional time with the ones you love or heck, even grab some "ME TIME," you are here for a reason. You know that there is a better way. A way that you can be more fulfilled, more productive, more organized and step into the greatest version of yourself.

Maybe you are organized right now but you want to manage your time better, maybe you are juggling a million different things and just want to find the systems and strategies to be more productive in the day, or maybe you just want to finally get your life in order. Hey, there is nothing wrong with any of that! We all start somewhere and we can always be improving, becoming better, and the best versions of ourselves means continually working on YOU. I'm proud of you for showing up here—for taking the first step and investing in yourself.

This book will walk you through everything, from how to step into the most productive version of yourself, how to get more done, become more organized, figure out your non-negotiables and those pesky time-suckers that take away our most valuable commodity–our time–and you will finally be able to step into the BEST version of yourself as a woman in business, wife or partner, mother, or a woman who just wants to feel more accomplished and get ISH done!

Women are AMAZING beings! We do it all and make it look easy! We take care of the home, our families, our work obligations, school obligations, and *still* seem to do it all happily for the ones we love and care about. What I want to share with you in this book is how to take all those overwhelming tasks, chores, housework, obligations, and to-do lists, and find a better system and strategy on how to get it all done. And not just DONE but getting to the end of your day and feeling accomplished, fulfilled, and living in your purpose. If that may seem like a dream come true or even too good to be true–I ask you to challenge yourself. Realize how amazing you are already, and if you take the trainings, systems, tips, and tools I give to you in this book and apply even a small percentage of what I share with you, I promise you will stop spinning your wheels day in and day out and finally achieve the goals you set out to accomplish for yourself.

But it's not magic–it's effort and a decision to start showing up for yourself! You will not only accomplish your goals, but you will accomplish them faster than you ever thought possible without feeling stressed and overwhelmed, and without neglecting or feeling guilty to the ones you love most. The key to all of this is *making a decision*—making the decision to go all in on YOU. When you feel accomplished, fueled up, and living on purpose, then everyone around you will see and feel that! I'm so excited for you to go on this journey with me. I encourage you to keep a journal or log as you read through this book. Journal about where you are now as you start, and journal as you begin implementing and making progress. When you get to the end of this book you will easily be able to see where transformations have been made.

I work with women of all walks of life, and EVERY TIME I hear the same thing—when I first meet with them they are stressed, overwhelmed, and feel like they never have enough time in the day. I'm so excited to finally get this into your hands so you can apply these systems and strategies and finally step into the power you've had all along! It's kind of like Dorothy in *The Wizard of Oz*. You have everything you need already within you, but you just need to know how to apply it, use it to your benefit, and create the life you've always dreamed of living.

Chapter 1 is about *WHY* I needed these systems so desperately in my own life and how a breakdown lead me to the biggest breakthrough of my life. This breakthrough was an incredible blessing in disguise and allowed me to not only have a massive transformation myself, but also led me to the incredibly impactful work I do today.

Chapter 2 reveals why I am so passionate about this and what my mission is for women all over the world. I believe when women are in control, living their most productive lives, it affects everyone around them, and they are able to step into their power to create the best version of themselves and live the life of their dreams.

Chapter 3 dives into Purpose Over Overwhelm. It's crucial for us as women to live on and in our purpose. When we are not fulfilled we become overwhelmed, stressed, and depressed. When you are living on purpose it means you are accomplishing what you set out to accomplish in this world. Some days that means getting all the kids out the door to school on time and other days it means slaying those big, juicy goals you have. No matter what your purpose is I want you to feel in control and able to step into your power and purpose without the feeling of stress and overwhelm. I will walk you through what this looks like and how you can focus on Purpose Over Overwhelm.

Chapter 4 covers Prioritizing Your time. Where your time is going, how much it is worth, and what are you doing right now to make the most out of the time you have. We all have the same twenty-four hours in the day, but how you show up, prioritizing and managing that time, is the difference between hitting your goals and being disappointed and falling short. This chapter is about how you can best prioritize your time so you can get the most done, be fulfilled, and feel accomplished at the end of each day.

Chapter 5 deep-dives into Time Management and How to Protect Your Time and Energy. We all have certain habits we turn to when we are stressed, overwhelmed, or bored. These dangerous habits keep you further away from achieving your goals each day, keeping you distracted, off task, and occupied with time-suckers that zap your precious time away. I will cover the science of how habits work, why you have these bad habits, and how to replace them with new ones that will allow you to ramp up your productivity and ultimately allow you to get closer to your goals each and every day.

Chapter 6 explains the importance of knowing your non-negotiables. This is critical in time management and the success of your work and home life. What you say YES and NO to drives whether you get closer or further away from those goals. I will help you focus on identifying your non-negotiables as well as put practices in place so it's easier for you to say YES to the things that will move you CLOSER to your goals and stay away from the time-suckers that will ultimately move you away from achieving your goals and dreams.

Chapter 7 takes you through Setting Systems into Place to Step into Your Success. I will guide you through the 3D system of three important D's in your life—Do It Yourself, Delegate, or Delete. I'll break down the practices of each one of these so you can better understand how to implement this system in your own business, home, and personal life. These systems become crucial as you take on more work, expand your business, grow your family, and ultimately want to get more done and feel accomplished day in and day out. You will journal on the 3D approach and start to see where in your own life you need to start making changes for a more peaceful, productive, and fulfilled life all around.

Chapter 8 reveals my own best practices on how to have a more organized home and work life. It is critical that both your home and work life are in a state where you can work and operate at optimal levels. This will create a more organized and peaceful environment for you, your business, and family to thrive in.

Chapter 9 is all about how to Take Back Control of Your Time and Reach Your Goals Sooner. With all of these practices in place, you will now be able to run your day instead of your day running you. If your days felt overwhelmed and stressed before, I will show you how taking back control of your time allows you to reach your goals sooner and become the best version of yourself for you and everyone around you. When YOU are fulfilled and living on purpose, life is sweeter, you feel less stressed, and you are the creator of your own destiny!

Chapter 10 wraps everything up with Stepping Into Your Power as a Woman Who Wants to Have It All. This is SO POSSIBLE! This is your life and you get to create it! It's your time to step into your power and greatness and have all the incredible things you desire. When you adopt all of these tools, systems, and strategies I share with you, then you *will* become UNSTOPPABLE! Look out, world, because you'll not only HAVE the power, you'll know how to use it! This chapter shows how all of these systems come together to allow you to live the life of your dreams as you implement all the skills and tools covered in the book.

This book will help you understand the importance of why you need the tools and strategies of time management and productivity in your life, but it will also show you how to use them wisely and in your own way. Take these tools and systems and implement them as you see fit in your own life. Don't get overwhelmed with too much too soon. Take on one chapter at a time and implement what's in it. See how that goes for you and change or modify based on your own wants and needs in your personal, work, and home life. So many of us go from day to day just surviving. I want this book to allow you to step into your power and thrive as the incredible woman you are. I can't wait for you to dive in, start implementing, and seeing the MAGIC that starts to happen as you step into your power, amp up your productivity, and create the life of your dreams! It's time to claim your power, so turn to the first chapter and let's get to work!

1
Breakdowns Bring Breakthroughs

Before we get into the tools, systems, and strategies of this book, I want to give you a little background on how I got to where I am today. You see, I wasn't always this super organized, productive, or operating at the levels I do now. It was a journey to get here. Growing up, I came from a home where my mom worked full time, raised three kids, and my dad was (and still is today) working and hustling as a successful entrepreneur. They worked together as a team, but this meant most days and nights my mom was (without ANY help) taking care of the home, helping my brother and I with homework and school projects, doing the laundry, trying to get dinner on the table, all while working a full-time job. And if you can even imagine it, this was pre-internet, before having access to podcasts, Google, and mentors at your fingertips through social media. She was just trying to SURVIVE! She spent her days putting out fires moment-to-moment and just trying to make it through getting us to bed most nights so she could breathe. I give her a lot of credit for truly doing all the things with no help at her disposal. This frantic state did bring on a lot of overwhelm and exhaustion.

I know so many of you women also struggle with the same feelings trying to juggle everything and just keep your head above water. You bite off more than you can chew. Many times you are trying to "balance" work life and home life. Many of you are also trying to do this all at the same time. This is a recipe for disaster, overwhelm, and burnout.

Here's the thing: That feeling of overwhelm and burnout is a *choice*. You get to choose at any time to step out of the burnout and into balance. You can choose to go from overwhelmed to living a life on purpose. This is possible! How do I know? Because I went through this myself. I was also on that journey of feeling overwhelmed, stressed, and wondering how could I possibly do all the things and get everything done I needed to do as a wife, mother, home-maker and businesswoman. There are so many hats to wear, and I was determined to crack the code on not just surviving each day but THRIVING.

Being frantic, unorganized, and overwhelmed is NOT a badge of honor. So many of us talk and walk around "hustling" as if this is something to be proud of. Now, while working and being efficient IS something to aspire to, a place of stress and overwhelm is not where creativity, love, and happiness grow. I know so many of you are overwhelmed, overworked, and truly in survival mode EVERY DAY.

Just as my mom was experiencing the stress and overwhelm in her days, growing up I remember thinking to myself, "There has to be a better way for her." I'd go over to friends' homes or babysit and I remember seeing systems, charts, and organizational tools implemented in the family. I've always loved systems and creativity, and remember thinking, "Wow, what a great concept!" Those homes always seemed to be less stressed, more organized, and efficient. I knew there had to be something to it. Little did I know it would be years later when I would actually create and implement my own systems to help moms, wives, and businesswomen all over the world step into their power and create similar systems for themselves.

Fast forward to after college and I had been working as a wedding and event planner for six years both in my own business and for a local golf club outside Philadelphia. As you can imagine when you handle the biggest day in someone's life, you better have your sh*t together! I loved wedding planning. I loved the whole process—the love story, the details, and the planning! Oh the planning! I had charts and systems to keep everything systematized and organized. It was one of my favorite parts of the business. The more organized I was and the more organization I brought into my business, the more fun I had. I realized early on how the more organized I was, the more productive and efficient I was. The more weddings I could take on, the more business I would close, which meant more money coming in. For me, wedding planning was a dream job. When I met my husband in 2013, I ended up leaving the industry and following my own love story. I left behind the brides and the business, ready to step into my new role and life in sunny Florida. I have to say wedding planning set me up for success in more ways than I ever imagined. I am so grateful for finding my passion in wedding planning but even more so for revealing my passion in systems, organization, and planning. This was just the beginning.

In 2016 I married the love of my life, Jarrod. In 2017 we started to expand our family and welcomed our first baby boy, Jacob. I took every class imaginable to prepare—every baby prep class, breastfeeding class, prenatal yoga, welcoming home baby, even baby CPR and First Aid. We hired a doula and learned about every possible scenario to be prepared. Well, baby class doesn't actually prepare you for what happens *after* taking the baby home, when you're running on zero sleep, exhausted from breastfeeding, being up all night, and of course all the fears you face as a first time mother AND trying to find what I've come to call "your new normal."

I thought I was prepared! I figured every baby class, babysitting since I was twelve, having a younger brother who I cared for at age eleven, and reading all the books would prepare me for this role. Boy, was

I in for a rude awakening! What they don't tell you in the books, classes, or in the doctor's office, is that life as you once knew it is over—forever! This isn't to mourn the past but to really take a good hard look at where you are now and realize you need to figure out a new plan. Work is no longer the same, your marriage changes (both in challenging ways and beautiful ways), your personal life changes, and every moment of your life is dependent upon this amazing new human being in your life. You now have to find your new normal and figure out what it means and looks like for you.

What happened next was a blessing in disguise. I had a breakdown. Yes, crying, sobbing on the bathroom floor (thank you postpartum hormones) about how I was going to get back to ME again. I was always an extremely motivated, ambitious, go-getting woman both in business and in life, but right in that moment I didn't even know how to pick myself up off the floor or find MY "new normal." This breakdown moment needed to happen. It was a sign. It was either my future self, or God, or my guardian angels looking over me and directing me.

I remember in that moment hearing a voice. The voice felt like an out-of-body experience. It was telling me everything was going to be OK and that this was a huge learning lesson—that I had something so powerful to learn from this. This wasn't a break*down*, this was a break*through*! I was going through this to learn something bigger. At that moment, I remember thinking, "Just take one small step at a time. Do one small thing to make progress each day." I couldn't expect my postpartum, new mommy self to be slaying dragons and putting out fires like I was used to doing pre-baby. But what I COULD DO was take baby steps each day to accomplish small wins for myself. This is where it all started.

Ask any new mom and she'll tell you she feels like she does a million things in a day, only to end the day feeling like she did nothing. As a new mom, this is the time when you need to be reveling in your baby—giving that little angel all the love and attention, and also taking care of YOU! Focusing on laundry, dishes, work, and whatever else needs to be done can all wait. I knew my time was spent now on my baby, taking care of myself, and resting when I could, but I also knew I could put an action plan in place to find my "new normal." I started off making myself what looked like a "chore chart" each day. This wasn't anything huge. The items on the list were simple, but they helped me conquer my day, which in turn helped me conquer my mindset, which then allowed me to eventually set myself up for my big, juicy goals once I was ready to take them on again. The things on this list were simple, such as make your bed, shower, get dressed, cook dinner. I wasn't moving mountains, I was finding ME again!

Once I was able to start finding myself again and my "new normal," I was able to start tracking these wins for myself. I went to bed every night with a plan, and I woke up every morning with a plan and purpose. What I started to notice as I was implementing these small changes every day was how over time I was feeling more accomplished, more fulfilled, and finally able to get back into my rhythm again. It didn't happen overnight—it was the compound effect of building on the success of each day that finally allowed me to find my groove. What I found was I didn't overwhelm myself with tasks or to-do lists that would be impossible for me to achieve. I focused on three things each day to move myself forward, and that's when I started seeing the magic happen.

I started implementing what I call my three overarching daily goals. This wasn't a to-do list or a wish list, this was a list of three things that were my non-negotiables each day I needed to accomplish. It was short and sweet but made a major difference in my life when it came to getting the things done I needed to accomplish each day. In the beginning, these three overarching daily goals were as simple as make the bed, make sure to eat at each meal, and put on makeup or get dressed. As I got further along on my postpartum journey, these overarching daily goals started to evolve. They went from making sure I was eating and fueling my body properly to getting out of the house, working out, and making time to intentionally connect with my husband. You see, having a to-do list is very different from an overarching daily goals list. To-do lists go on and on, and you're never really sure where you should be putting your attention. With an overarching daily goals list, you know your focus goes to three things you are prioritizing that day—no more, no less. Once you complete these three things, you feel accomplished and have a very clear direction on what you need to conquer that day.

Your overarching daily goals give you direction and focus, and allow you to feel like you've mastered your day. Once you complete those three overarching daily goals, which are the priority that day, you can then move on to anything else you want to focus on. Keep in mind these three overarching daily goals change from day to day, but they should be the three most important tasks you need to get done that day to feel fulfilled and accomplished.

I want you to start implementing this in your own life. Before you go to bed each night, you should have a planner or just a simple notebook you can use. Write down the night BEFORE what your three overarching daily goals are for the next day. You can also write out a tentative schedule on how your day is going to look. I plan out from the moment I wake up until when I go to bed. Keep in mind your schedule is flexible and it can change (more than likely it will). Your schedule is just to give you an idea of what your day looks like, how you envision your day going, and then you work around the edits and changes as needed. Your focus, however, is ALWAYS on your three overarching daily goals. That list is your guiding light, and the only thing you need to worry about. Do this and you will set yourself up for a successful day, week, month, and a whole lifetime of productivity, clarity, and hitting your targets and goals both in your personal and professional life.

Everything changed for me when I was able to implement these systems. My days became highly productive, I was happier, and felt more accomplished. Not only that, but it had a ripple effect on my family and business. More work was accomplished, I became a happier wife and mother, and I truly felt fulfilled in each area of my life.

As I've worked with countless women in this space, they tell me when they first come to me how they are completely overwhelmed and exhausted. I know it's because there are no systems or organization. Once you can tap into this system I'm sharing with you, then you open up the doors for more time, energy, and happiness in your life! You start to experience what it's like to be able to show up 100% in each area so you don't feel run down, disorganized, and frantic each day. My hope and wish is that every burnt-out, stressed-out wife, mama, and businesswoman can get her hands on this book with the tools and systems to step out of a life of being overwhelmed and into a life of happiness, productivity, and organization. I promise, this is a life-changing experience if you decide to tap into the tools and systems in this book. You, your family, and your business deserve it!

In the space below, write down a moment or experience you felt was a breakdown but afterwards realized was a breakthrough:

_____
_____
_____
_____

How did you take the moment and learn something powerful from it?

_____
_____
_____
_____

How did you come out better from the experience? What was the lesson learned?

_____
_____
_____
_____

Key Takeaways & Notes:

2
Helping Success-Minded Women Be the Best Version of Themselves

Now that you have a little backstory on me, how I started and transitioned into my professional career, and the success and impact productivity and time management made on my life, I want to share with you WHY I am so passionate about these topics and subjects, and how MASSIVE an impact this change can make in your own life.

As I mentioned, I experienced first-hand in my life how huge an impact being organized and managing your time effectively helps to create a more balanced, organized, and fulfilled life. I saw personally in my own family and for myself how stress, overwhelm, and anxiety can creep in when you lead a life without systems and structures in place. Once I became a mother, the meaning of time management and productivity took on a whole new meaning. Before kids, if I put off writing an email, making an important phone call, or running errands that needed to get done, I could always "do it later." As a mom, there's ALWAYS one more thing to do around the house, dinner to cook, laundry to get done, little people (or a husband) to attend to. As moms, we tend to put our priorities and ourselves on the backburner. After my son Jacob was born, I realized there is no "dabbling" in motherhood. You're ALL IN, fast and furious, and you better be a quick learner. As the productive businesswoman I was used to being with my career, I soon realized I could start to apply the same habits and teachings to motherhood just as I did in business. But now this looked very different. I had to become laser-focused on my goals, targets, and what I wanted to accomplish each and every day.

In the beginning of my postpartum journey, those goals were as "simple" as getting dressed, taking a shower, and putting on makeup that day. After a while of getting down the basics and moving into post-postpartum, my targets and goals started to evolve. I started seeing major wins (and FAST) both in my business and in my personal life. I started taking my time management, organization, and productivity hacks and applying them across the board in my life—professionally and personally and it was a GAME-CHANGER! I started tracking what EXACTLY I was doing, the plan I was following, the systems I was implementing, and the WINS I was having. I quickly realized if this could have such a major impact on me and my own family, it would be worth seeing if the same teachings could help other moms and businesswomen.

When I first started offering these systems and coaching to women, I wanted to test it out and see if it would actually apply to others. After a few weeks of testing these systems and strategies, the results were in! Not only were these women feeling more accomplished and less stressed, but they were also feeling more fulfilled across the board. These strategies applied to *everyone* who implemented them! Single women in business, wives, mothers, working moms, stay-at-home moms, moms who worked from home—it was a GAME-CHANGER across the board. The common denominator? These women were ready for change! They were tired of being tired and wanted a solution—just like I wanted when I started creating and implementing this for myself. The women who experienced massive wins were COMMITTED! They learned, implemented, and then watched as the magic unfolded in their businesses, their families, and of course for themselves.

I am so passionate about what I teach and coach on time management, organization, implementing systems, and productivity because I've seen over and over again the SUCCESS of how IT WORKS! This approach changes lives! This allows the overworked, overwhelmed business babe to get organized, expand her business, make more money, and truly play at levels she deserves. I've seen this work for busy moms juggling work life and home life. They come to me and say they are so thankful after so many years of feeling burnt-out and overwhelmed because they finally can breathe and feel like they can get a grasp on "doing all the things."

The systems and strategies I am going to teach you and walk you through work! They have been proven time and time again, but I am only going to ask one thing of you: I ask you to COMMIT. I ask you to commit to this process of learning and IMPLEMENTING. You can watch a training, webinar, or take a class, but if you never implement what you learn you will always be wondering what went wrong and why it didn't work for you. Just like any good exercise plan, IT works when YOU work. The same applies here. If you're ready to step into your power, get rid of feeling overwhelmed, overworked, exhausted, and are ready to implement the systems, tools and the strategies I have for you, then I am so excited and ready for you to truly feel accomplished and live a fulfilled life in every area you crave. All it takes is the moment where you DECIDE you are going to commit. Lose the excuses! Stop syaing "I can't" or "I don't have enough time" or whatever other excuses you've used in the past that ultimately stand in the way of YOUR SUCCESS. When you implement all of the tools I will provide to you, only then will you truly step into your greatness and power.

Right now I want you to anticipate what may stand in your way of getting to where you want to be. Is it the feeling of not being good enough? Are you going to tell yourself you don't have time? Are you going to let laziness, disorganization, and other bad habits creep back in? By anticipating what may get in the way of your success, you can troubleshoot now and avoid falling into the "victim trap" once you begin. By knowing and acknowledging any weaknesses or excuses that may come up, you can be ready to spot them when they arise. It will be easier to stay on track if you can notice where and when you may fall off the game plan.

If you are truly committed to becoming the best version of you for your family, business, and YOURSELF, then it's time to get serious about how you will take action. Don't let minor setbacks get in your way. Instead, put the plan in place now as to what you will do IF (more like when) you experience a setback. It takes on average about twenty to thirty days to form a new habit. Within that formation period you will want to make excuses. Your mind will play tricks on you to do everything it can to suck you back into its comfort zone. Stay strong, my friend! You can do this, and I promise you the payoff is so beautiful on the other side! You no longer have to fall victim to overwhelm, stress, chaos, and feeling burnout every day. This system works when you do, and you are the only one who can control where you are going next.

If you have to get visual and creative, then go for it. Print out images, inspiring words or quotes on how you want to feel and what you want your life to look like. Print them out, put them up as reminders on your mirror, in your car, make them the wallpaper on your desktop or phone. Whatever you need to do to reach this goal, DO IT! Living a life that is more organized and productive, where you are in total control, is such a blessing. Your life will change, evolve, and get better just by taking these steps and implementing them in your life. Like I said, there is no big secret to this—it's simply about commitment, following the steps, and deciding you are making a change NOW!

My mission is to help every single stressed-out, tired, overworked, frustrated, overwhelmed business babe, wife, and mother step into her power and OWN each area of her life. Own her time, her day, her decisions, and start operating from a place of abundance, happiness, and fulfillment. Life doesn't have to be one big NASCAR race, racing from one thing to the next. You CAN feel accomplished, fulfilled, and successful in each area of your life, but you have to own it! It's time for you to *Slay Your Day* and start implementing all the tools and techniques for you to tap into your power!

I can't wait to go on this journey with you! Let's get started!

In what area(s) of your life do you feel most stressed out now?

_____
_____
_____
_____

If you could get control of this area(s), how would it make you feel?

_____
_____
_____
_____

On a scale of 1-10, how committed are you to making this change? Why?

_____
_____
_____
_____

Key Takeaways & Notes:

3
Trading Overwhelm for Purpose

Tell me if this sounds familiar: The feeling of being worn down, distracted, and living a life where you are unfulfilled because you are constantly OVERWHELMED. You see and feel the chores, tasks, and to-do lists pile up day after day only to become worn down and stressed out by the monotony and tasks at hand. I know it can feel overwhelming, exhausting, and impossible at times to get ahead or even make any progress. It doesn't have to be this way.

I want to help change this for you! I want to show you how you can take the life you are living now, with the same tasks and to do lists, and create a life of purpose and passion.

The reason why you are so bogged down day after day is because you're not able to relish in the WINS of the day. The feeling of accomplishment and productivity allows you to be more creative, find your passions, and live a purpose-filled life. Unfortunately, with the overwhelming demands of life and the hectic lives we tend to live, all contribute to feeling overworked and overwhelmed. When you are in this space it's impossible to feel like you're living your life on purpose. Rather, you just feel stressed and like your days are running you. I'm going to help you change that! I want to help you step into your power and start racking up wins day after day so you create a winning cycle you can feel good about.

Ever experience those days when you just feel like superwoman? You get all the work done you need to get done, the house is clean (or picked up), the laundry is done, you made dinner, and you just feel like a freaking rock star? How often does this happen for you? Are those days few and far between. or is this the regular for you? I want you to know you can have this all the time. This doesn't need to be a once-in-a-blue-moon special. When you're operating your life in an organized, productive and methodical manner, days like that happen again and again. You feel like you're on top of the world, you feel like you are in a state of flow and have energy and excitement! Wouldn't it be great to live like that all the time? Here's a little secret: You CAN!

But you have to make the decision to stop overwhelming yourself with things you can't control or just can't control right now. When we can live in your purpose every day and step out of the overwhelm, when you decide what's important, what you are going to focus on now and what you can control, you authentically step into your power and purpose. You shouldn't be bogging yourself down with to-do lists that can never be accomplished or never-ending lists. As I mentioned, you want to start setting yourself up for success! So what does that look like? I'm glad you asked...let's dive in!

For starters, to-do lists and checklists are no longer your friend. What I want you to focus on now are two things: First, I want you every day to focus on the three most important things you want to achieve that day. As I mentioned before, these are your *three overarching daily goals*. These three tasks help you to move the ball forward each day. These three tasks get your undivided attention and are at the forefront of your priority list. Everything else is just a bonus!

Second, write out your schedule for the next day the night BEFORE. This allows you to go to bed knowing what you need to accomplish and waking up with a game plan in place. This is a great time to do a brain dump of all the things you need to accomplish the next day. Ever try to go to bed when your mind is just racing with the things you need to do, remember, and accomplish the next day? Take that worry off your plate by writing out your schedule for the next day and adding in a brain dump of anything you need to remember or pay attention to the next day. I promise this will help you sleep better and not stay up all hours of the night thinking about what you need to accomplish the next day and hoping you remember in the morning (been there, done that—never again!).

Keep in mind your schedule is in place to guide you as to what you need to get done that day. This is to help keep you on track but ONLY so you have an idea of what needs to get done, and where your attention gets to go AFTER those three important things on your overarching daily goals list are accomplished. By staying focused on the things you ARE accomplishing and putting attention on the wins each day, you will be able to get more done, feel more fulfilled, and start living your life ON PURPOSE.

It's such a game-changer when you start operating your time, schedule, and days from a place of purpose. You get more done, have more energy, fuel the people around you, and truly feel like you can "do it all!" By focusing on the wins, you create a winning mentality. It takes stacking these wins day after day to create the confidence you want to have in yourself. This confidence radiates everywhere,– in your business, your home, your loved ones, and most importantly in yourself. So many women beat themselves up for the things they don't accomplish that day or the tasks they didn't get to. Well, we're changing this mentality! I want you to start focusing on the things you *are* accomplishing and the wins you *are* having.

Let's start right now. What are some accomplishments you can give yourself a pat on the back for right now, in this moment? Got out of bed? Got dressed? Got the kids off to school? Got your workout in? Sent work emails out? Connected with new clients? Did some prospecting in your business? Got dinner on the table? No win is too small, and you need to start acknowledging yourself for what you ARE accomplishing rather than focusing on beating yourself up over what you didn't get to today. The more you focus on what you DID accomplish and the wins you DID achieve, the greater motivation and drive you will have for getting more done and becoming more productive. If this concept is new to you, start off small. Place reminders of your wins around your home, office, or even on your phone. Remind yourself of the powerful boss babe you are—the one who is in total control, slays it in business, at home, and SLAYS HER DAY!

Now, not every day will be perfect. If you're having an off day, I want you to look at the things that DID go right. You got out of bed, you showered you, made dinner for the family—whatever it is you can focus on that's positive—that's where your attention goes. This will help create the pattern of more wins and more success to keep coming!

Life happens, right? You get sick, the kids get sick, unexpected things come up at work. But just know that when everything seems like it's out of control, you can still control one thing: *How you respond*. You get to control how you react and respond to each situation. You can respond with overwhelm, anxiety, and stress or you can respond calm, cool, and collected knowing this is also in your control. Control the controllable. Living a life of purpose over overwhelm means you are in control. You are the captain of your ship and you decide where it goes. The more you remain in control of your time, day, and how you respond is what allows you to step into a place of power and purpose. You get to decide where and how you show up, what you say yes (and no) to, and what you put on your plate. If you feel like your plate is starting to get too full, start saying NO to events, people, and obligations that don't serve you. You cannot operate at the highest, most fulfilled, purpose-driven version of yourself if you are stressed out, worried, and frantic all the time.

You step into purpose over overwhelm one decision at a time. What are the goals you are going after? Who are the people who bring you the most joy? What activities bring you the most happiness? You want to focus on those. Focus on knowing the more of a hold you have on your own day, time, and priorities the better you get to show up for everyone else. This goes for your business, personal life, and taking care of yourself.

I challenge you to take an inventory of your day, activities, and commitments right now. What is causing you to feel frantic and overwhelmed and what is allowing you to feel joy, fulfillment, and purpose? Make a list. Do a big brain dump of all the things you are no longer going to engage in, the things you can pass off to someone else, or the things you can delete off your plate (I call this the 3D system, and I'll go deeper into this in chapter 7). Now, I want you to focus on the things that bring you joy and allow you to step into your full power and potential. How do you feel? How do you operate when you are in this state? Does it allow you to feel accomplished and show up as the best version of yourself? If you are living in a state of purpose over overwhelm, then the answer should be yes.

Always remember you are in control of you. You get to say yes (and more importantly no) to the things your heart desires. You get to choose to live in purpose over overwhelm and it's simply just making the decision to do so. Make this a conscious decision each day until it becomes a habit. Take note of the people, places, and things that bring you joy. Fuel your life with more of that! You will know when you are operating from a place of PURPOSE OVER OVERWHELM when your days are organized, they are structured, and you feel like you are moving the ball forward each day.

If you feel like you are slipping back into bad habits/behaviors, always remember to go back to the basics—focusing on the three most important tasks of the day. When you live your life from a place of purpose, the creativity flows, you're vibing high and you feel like you can do it all (which YOU CAN). Keep in mind this isn't about doing it all at ONCE (which is impossible). There are smart ways to multitask and inefficient ways to multitask (more on that later). When you focus on controlling the controllable, you are able to truly banish the stress and anxiety in your life, and even when life around you may feel frantic you know you've got this! You control how much you take on, what you say yes to, what you say no to, and everything in between. Do not take on commitments that will make you feel guilty about having to do them later. Living on purpose means living a life where you are in control of your ship. That stats here and now, TODAY. Step into your power and claim your power so you can live a life on PURPOSE and banish the overwhelm.

How do you know when you are living your life on purpose and not overwhelm? It will be extremely clear to you when you tap into your purpose. I have clients I work with who come to me super stressed, overworked, and overwhelmed, but by the time they get into the groove of our coaching together, or my courses, programs, and so on, I can hear it in their voices. I hear raving testimonials from working women, moms, and single boss babes who go from overwhelmed to fueled, organized, and living on purpose! These women go from telling me they are run-down with "not enough time in the day" to having more than enough time in the day to get EVERYTHING done. They feel like they're living in a whole new world of organization with systems and strategies that allow them to be fulfilled in every area as moms, wives, and businesswomen, all while having enough time for themselves.

I work with solopreneurs who go from run-down and exhausted, spinning their wheels in their business, to building teams and systems to maximize their time, productivity, efficiency, and effectiveness in their business. ANYONE CAN DO THIS! There are no secrets or magic tricks these women have that you don't. It's just a matter of getting serious about where you are, how you feel, and how badly you want to make a change. "Nothing changes if nothing changes." So I want you to commit now to YOU. Putting these systems in place not only makes you better in business, but you become more powerful and effective at home, how you show up for others, and most importantly, how you take care of and show up for yourself.

The time is NOW. Implement the steps and tips from these chapters and watch the ripple effect of how living in your purpose versus overwhelm radiates throughout your life, to all the people you love and care about, and how much of a difference this makes across all aspects of your life. I can't wait to hear YOUR success story!

Where do you feel overwhelmed now?

_____
_____
_____
_____
_____

Make a list of all the things you are no longer going to engage in and what no longer serves you:

_____
_____
_____
_____
_____

What are the people, places, and activities that bring you joy?

_____
_____
_____
_____
_____

Key Takeaways & Notes:

4
How Much Is Your Time Worth?

So many of us are busy working women, wives, mothers, and usually wearing multiple hats (at once). More than ever you need to be prioritizing your time now. I want you to start to think of your time as money. What are the investments each day you want to be pouring into? Keep in mind, every day this can change, but this will help you gauge HOW much time you are pouring into any one area, or person. This allows you to start to think about how you truly prioritize your time. You realize certain tasks take far longer than they should and certain people probably take up more time than you'd like, but this helps you start to really focus in on getting more done and being with the people you truly want to be with.

I know for most of us, being in our business 24/7 doesn't sound like fantasy land but also, being with our kids/family and friends all day long we wouldn't have a business either. This is all about finding the right "balance" for you, your business and what YOUR ideal life looks like. Want to know the good news? You get to create this! You get to keep creating this, choosing the lifestyle you want to live and show up where you want to show up. I'm going to walk you through a few exercises that allow you to step into making big moves in your business but will also allow you to show up exactly how you want in each area of your life.

To start off, I want you to identify what an "IDEAL" day looks like to you. I want you to think of everything here. How many hours are you sleeping at night? How many hours are you in your business, with your kids, investing in yourself with self-care or with friends. It's important to start off with what your IDEAL day looks like so we can work backwards from there. After you do this fun exercise, I want you to start looking at your days as they are now. Where are the gaps? Are you spending more time in your business than you'd like? Or maybe you're not spending enough time on your business or on yourself. The important part of this exercise is to understand that in order to get as close to your ideal day as possible we need to start looking at the *targets, goals, and money making moves* in your business that will move you forward each day so you CAN be present in these other areas.

I want to talk about "mom guilt" for a moment. Not everyone reading this is a mom, but I am and I feel like this is an important note to include right now. I do want to point out that a lot of the times when we feel "mom guilt" are when we are working on overload and feel too much guilt being away from our kids/family, or the opposite is true—when we are with our kids we feel this pull and guilt about not being in our businesses. First, I want to assure you EVERY mom feels this way at one point or another, but what really helps me show up 100% in each area of my life is to actually BE in the moment or the thing I am in. If I'm in mommy mode, I'm not trying to take on important work emails, calls, and so on. The same is true when I'm working. At that time, my work or clients have my undivided attention.

It's crucial to know that (whether you're a mom or not) multitasking actually does you more harm than good. It's a proven fact that multitasking reduces efficiency and performance because our brains can only focus on one thing at a time. When we try and do two things at once (play with our kids, send out an email, take an important work call, all at the same time), your brain lacks the capacity to perform both tasks successfully. So whatever task or job you are in, be 100% in that. Finish it completely and then move on to the next thing. This will actually help you get more done quicker, and then move on to the next thing you want to put your full attention on.

Back to your ideal day: Once you've created your ideal day, start to audit your days and where you're actually spending time. Can you put focused attention on activities now to get them done more effectively than before? I also want you to note what your most productive activities are. These are the "money-making moves" I was talking about before. What are the activities in your business you know will make the most impact and income? Maybe for you this is prospecting, sending out emails, or creating new content. Whatever it is for you, go through your past month of activities to identify which ones had the most impact and ROI (return on investment).

On the other hand, what were the activities, distractions, or disruptions that took you further away from your goals and ideal day? Maybe it's notifications on your phone, maybe it's not batching out your work and bouncing from task to task with no set plan in place. Whatever it is for you, it's important to identify BOTH of these beneficial and harmful moves in your business and personal life so you are able to do more of what moves the ball forward and makes you happy versus your time-suckers and energy-draining tasks.

As I mentioned above, it's important to understand how getting as close to your ideal day as possible requires looking at the *targets, goals and money-making moves*. We spoke about how you identify your money-making moves, but let's talk about targets and goals. They are both very different, and I want you to be able to identify the difference so you can start making an impact on the progress and productivity of your day.

Your goals are the big juicy things you go after. Examples might include writing a book, launching your podcast, hitting a certain financial milestone, and so on. Your targets are the smaller micro-steps that help you get there. Examples of these might be writing for an hour a day until the book is done, doing research to launch your podcast, making a certain number of phone calls or prospecting each day. Keep in mind you want to be very specific when you set these micro-targets. Think about setting S.M.A.R.T micro targets to get to your bigger goals. If you haven't seen this before, S.M.A.R.T is an acronym for SPECIFIC, MEASURABLE, ATTAINABLE, REALISTIC, and TIMELY. When you want to reach a goal, you will reach it much faster when you can create the micro-targets around hitting you goal when you set S.M.A.R.T targets. This allows you to hit your goals on time (or even sooner than expected), not overwhelm yourself in the process, and focus on what needs to get done that is right in front of you to move the ball forward.

When you ask someone about their goals, they typically like to aim high and tell you all these grandiose ideas and dreams they have without a plan in place. S.M.A.R.T targets allow you to identify the goal and get laser-focused on how you will achieve it. Let me give you an example of what a S.M.A.R.T goal looks like versus any other regular goal. Setting any type of "regular" goal would look like: "I want to get fit" or "I want to lose weight." As you can see, there is nothing SPECIFIC, MEASURABLE, ATTAINABLE, REALISTIC or TIMELY about this goal.

A better way to structure a S.M.A.R.T goal would be, "I am going to drink sixty ounces of water a day, eat clean seven days a week, and workout five times a week for a minimum of forty minutes to lead a healthy lifestyle." As you can see with this S.M.A.R.T goal we are very SPECFIC about how we will get to this goal with ATTAINABLE steps. There are MEASURABLE action steps in place that are REALISTIC to achieve and TIMELY based on the time stamp on the goal.

Set yourself up to win by creating S.M.A.R.T goals that will be easy for you to achieve. As they become easier for you and you incorporate them into your lifestyle and your daily habits, then you can add in more days or time as needed. Start small and do not overwhelm yourself. You can always add on more, but make sure you never try to take on too many changes at once. When you put S.M.A.R.T goals in place, you can easily see how using this system will set you up for success and help you to actually achieve the goals you are going after! If you're ready to stop making excuses, get out of your own way, and start making major changes in your life, setting S.M.A.R.T goals is the best place to start!

Why is mapping out your ideal day, identifying your time-suckers, and setting S.M.A.R.T targets so important? Because at the end of the day you want to create a life and a lifestyle you actually enjoy. So many women I talk to and who start off coaching with me, tell me they feel drained and exhausted, and not just at the end of the day—the feel this way all the time. This is because they feel like they are spinning their wheels day after day and never actually accomplishing anything.

When you have a plan in place, when you know your worth, and when you realize how much your time is worth, then you stop wasting time on the not-so-important things and start focusing your time and energy on the things that really matter. I want you to start to see how much value you bring and how much value you have! This is for the working boss babe, the stay at home mom, the supportive wife, and for the woman who may wear many of these hats. What you bring to the table is so valuable. Where you choose to spend your time is where you are investing your money. Where you choose to show up tells people what is important to you. I want you to think of your day/time as money. Wherever you are investing your time, you are investing your money. What are the tasks, people, or things you are investing in now you feel are not returning enough value to you. What is your ROI on your activities, relationships, and everywhere you show up? Once you start to see how valuable this is, how valuable YOU ARE, you will start choosing what and who you spend your time on more wisely.

I know this may sound a little intense in the beginning, but the more you value your time, the more others will too. The more you show up for yourself and know where your priorities lie, the easier it will be to decide where your time goes, who you say yes/no to, and what you are available for. I know for me in my own life I am very strategic about my days, where my time goes, and even how much time I show up for something. I invest in meaningful relationships, learning and growing personally and professionally, showing up 100% in my business and for my clients. I also prioritize and make it a non-negotiable for me to invest and have time for self-care.

I know to some this may sound impossible to have ENOUGH time in the day, week, month, or even year to fit all of that in. But the truth of the matter is this: When you know your priorities, you no longer have time for time-suckers. Instead, you are able to identify them immediately and start putting your focus on the things that truly matter. This is one of the first steps in getting control over your time, freedom, and life. Put yourself in the driver's seat, take the wheel, and finally exercise control over all the things that come your way. Every choice you is an investment decision about your time, so make sure it's what you really want and what will truly serve you and your bigger purpose.

Map out what your ideal day looks like:

_____
_____
_____
_____

What are the activities, distractions, or disruptions that take you further away from your goals and ideal day:

_____
_____
_____
_____

What will you put your focus on NOW (tasks/people) that truly matter?

_____
_____
_____
_____

Key Takeaways & Notes:

5
Protect Your Time

To start off, I want to dive into what exactly is time management and why is it so important? Good time management allows you to accomplish more in a shorter period of time. This allows you to take advantage of investing in more of the things you want to do. This can be anything from investing in opportunities for growth, time with your family, in your business, and even on your own mental health and wellbeing. When you have good time management skills, this allows you to lead your day with intentional focus, lowers your stress levels, allows you to be in more control of your day, helps you focus more, and have a clear outlook on the things you need to say yes and no to. Good time management ultimately boils down to making your time and days run more smoothly, and who doesn't want that?

I work with countless women who, when they first come to me, feel overwhelmed and stressed in their days, they feel like they are on the never ending hamster wheel of work, family obligations, stress, and running around like crazy only to feel worn out and stressed out at the end of the day. THIS is NOT good time management. The woman who is in control of her time controls everything around her. She is the productivity queen and is in control of everything that comes her way, and can manage it like a BOSS! Time management is so crucial because it allows you to start your day off with clarity, allows you to focus on those high-level money-making moves we talked about, ends procrastination, puts your focus in one area to see it through until completion, and lowers your stress levels. Doesn't that sound like something we all want to have? So many of you are just worn out and drained by the end of the day you can't even imagine adding one more thing to your plate. What if I told you that if you added just one more step to your day you could increase your productivity automatically by 50%! By doing this one thing, you could reduce your stress, feel more accomplished, and start to get control of your days! Want to know what that little secret is?

I've mentioned it already, but this (not so little) secret is writing your planner/goals out the night before. Before you go to bed every night, I want you to take five minutes and brainstorm what your day will look like for the next day. It doesn't have to be an exact minute-by-minute breakdown but just a general idea of what you need to accomplish the next day. Here is where the REAL magic comes in. After you write out your rough schedule, you want to then focus on three overarching daily goals for the day that will help you move the ball forward with the tasks on your to-do list. Ultimately, these three overarching daily goals you are writing down each day are targets. These targets allow you to get closer to your big, juicy goals you set for yourself.

So what are the benefits of time management? We already spoke about why it's so crucial to implement this in your life, but I want you to take a closer look at the benefits. When you have a clear idea of how you will actually benefit from getting serious and putting these systems into place, you will be more eager to start! Here is a short run-down of just a few of the benefits you can expect when you start implementing good time management skills:

- You're more productive (both at work and at home).
- You have less stress and anxiety.
- You can take on and say yes to more opportunities.
- You notice personal and professional career growth.
- You have better quality relationships because you get to show up 100% in your relationships (without being distracted).
- You provide better quality work.
- You procrastinate less.
- You can finally enjoy "me time".

> You get to show up 100% in every area of your life.
> You are fulfilled and start living a life ON purpose.

As you can see there are so many benefits both personally and professionally when it comes to getting your time management in order!

I want you to look at how you use your time now. Do you procrastinate and push things off, only to be overwhelmed and stressed later? Or are you a planner—someone who schedules out her days, appointments, meetings? If you are in the former I want you to take an inventory of your day, kind of like what you would do if you were tracking your calories for the day if you were on a diet. Track everything you do for twenty-four hours. How much time are you spending on social media, meeting up for lunch, or coffee dates? What about how much time are you spending going back and forth replying to emails? When you do your twenty-four-hour time log, you will start to notice what things are taking up way too much of your time. A quick five minutes here and ten minutes there of procrastination, checking emails, or social media too often during the day adds up. Imagine if you had an extra hour in the day. What would you do with it? I can guarantee that once you start your time log and pay attention to where those time-suckers are creeping in, you'll start to eliminate them sooner and get back much more time in your day.

It all seems so harmless, but all of these little things take up time and energy in your day. You are wasting so much valuable time just by not paying attention to what you do day-to-day. Wouldn't it be amazing to actually GAIN time back in your day? You hear people say all the time how they "don't have enough time" or "I wish I had more hours in the day." This exercise is how you take back control. Time is one of the only commodities that once it's gone, it's gone FOREVER. How we spend our time dictates what's important to us. Meaning if we spend more time on work than with our kids, we are showing them where our priorities lie. The same is true vice versa–spending all our time with our kids and not enough time investing in our businesses, significant other, friendships, and personal time. It's a delicate balance, but the good news is that YOU are IN CONTROL.

After you take inventory of your day I want you to make sure you are including all the activities you do in twenty-four hours. This includes sleep, showering, work time, bathroom time, family time, personal time–EVERYTHING goes into this log. After you have your breakdown of your twenty-four hours of both the activity and how much time you've spent on the activity, I want you to figure out where you're spending too much time on activities that aren't either making you money or bringing you happiness. To be truly fulfilled means we are doing something we love but also making a difference and an impact.

What are some of those activities that would make sense to combine? A good example of this would be running errands. You don't want to start your day off running errands, have more to do in the middle of the day, and then have some in the evening. Batch out the tasks you have in a day so you can get more done. Even more than batching out your days, you want to start focusing on batching out your weeks. Certain days should have certain tasks. Wear your creative content creation hat on Mondays, your video shooting/editing days on Tuesdays, client meetings Wednesdays/Thursdays, and any in-person meetings on Fridays. This is just a quick example of how you can stay "in the zone" and get more done in one day than trying to wear ten different hats at once in your business all day long.

The same goes for at home. Once you do your time log and see you are spending precious time going from activity to activity, batch out your day so you create more time. A great example of this would be going to the grocery store on Sundays (or even betting using a food delivery system), meal prepping on Mondays and Wednesdays, cleaning on Tuesdays and Thursdays, having certain days for running errands, laundry, and even playdates. Know what needs to get done and use this system to your advantage to sensibly batch tasks together to create more time.

It's also important to mention here how there are activities and habits keeping you STUCK. Yes, that innocent text from your mom or the ping on your computer from the emails coming in are all hindering your productivity. Every time your attention is diverted from a task it takes another forty minutes to get re-engaged. Imagine being in the zone and working productively when someone comes in and interrupts you, or you get a phone call or look down and see a text from your husband. ALL of that takes you off-track and out of the work-flow zone of productivity. It's so important to know what habits are keeping you stuck! I like to stay in the work-flow zone by working with my phone on airplane mode. Turn off your notifications and work in a room or place where you have limited distractions so you can truly work in full productivity mode.

Another important point to mention is how some of the habits keeping you stuck aren't just distractions or disruptions. They can be trying to multitask, a disorganized work space, work socializing, meetings without purpose, or even the social media trap. Identify and know what your distractions look like. The clearer you are on pinpointing what they are, the more aware you will be when you fall into the trap and can get yourself out. At the end of the day these are all bad habits you want to kick to the curb so they do not disrupt your life and prevent you from accomplishing your goals.

Here are a few tips on how to beat those bad habits so you can fully step into the most productive version of yourself and conquer your time management once and for all:

1. *Choose a substitute for your bad habit:* When you want to grab your phone and scroll aimlessly through social media, substitute the habit of going for a walk, reading a book, or jumping on a call with a friend.
2. *Understand what triggers your bad habit:* If the first thing you do when you get into work is chat and mingle with coworkers, avoid the break room and put a new pattern of behavior in place. Start coming in to work and checking emails or jumping on client calls. Change up the pattern—make it easier on yourself to break the bad habits by avoiding them all together.
3. *Get an accountability buddy:* Pair up with someone and hold each other accountable. Knowing someone else expects you to deliver and be better is a powerful motivator.
4. Surround yourself with people who live the way you want to live: When you do this, it makes getting to the goal much more attainable as the habits you want to create are the norm of the people you surround yourself with.

5. *Do a review when you have a setback:* If you find yourself falling back into the bad patterns/habits, forgive yourself and keep aware that it happens. This doesn't mean you've failed, it means you're human. Forgive yourself and get back on track!

Another great exercise to work with to amp up your productivity is to group all your tasks into priority buckets, which is my little twist on what is better known as the Eisenhower Matrix invented by president Dwight D. Eisenhower. These buckets look like this:

- Urgent & Important
- Important but Not Urgent
- Urgent but Not Important
- Neither Urgent or Important

Identify which of these buckets your tasks fall into. You want to try and stay away from the urgent and important bucket because this means something was forgotten or this is an urgent "red light" task you need to put attention on. Ideally, you are setting a system in place day-to-day like we talked about, so you DON'T have anything end up in this bucket. This bucket would be more for emergencies or last-minute tasks that were forgotten and need urgent and immediate attention. A few examples of Urgent & Important would be deadlines that need to be met ASAP, urgent requests from customers or boss, signing new contracts, important meetings with tight deadlines, or putting out fires and handling complaints from angry customers. Think "code red emergency" for the Urgent & Important bucket.

The majority of everything else will fall into one of the other three buckets. Important tasks at home or work can fall into the "Important but not urgent" bucket. This means these tasks or items are important to put attention on and get done. If you are working your planner correctly like we talked about, where you are planning out your schedule and goals daily you will be able to keep most tasks and "to-do" in the rest of these three categories. An example of Important but Not Urgent would be planned-out projects, scheduling, research, creative design, or relationship building. These are the thing that are important but do not have a rapid deadline approaching.

Next is Urgent but Not Important. These are the things that could pop up in your day and cause distractions or take you off-track from how you planned your day. Urgent but Not Important tasks are the things preventing you from achieving your goals. I like to look at this bucket and see where I can reschedule or delegate what falls in this category. One of the biggest things that can fall into this category is distractions from other people. People asking you questions and small talk taking up too much of your valuable time. It's ok to just say "no" to people politely when you need to stay on track and focus on what IS important for you.

Some examples that fall into this category include random phone calls, people walking into your office, emails popping in all throughout the day, requests from family, co-workers, friends, and all kinds of trivial interruptions. Try and limit these urgent but not important pop-ups throughout the day by having a barrier system in place. Have a system where you implement only checking and responding to emails at certain times during the day and silencing your phone or putting it in airplane mode when working. I even have a little sign outside my home office when I'm working so when I'm in the work zone I am not going to be disrupted. Do what you need to do to put the barriers in place to protect your time and efficiency. You will get your work done much faster and more efficiently when you are fully focused and not having to worry about these urgent but unimportant matters that tend to pop up throughout the day.

Finally, we have Neither Urgent or Important. We want to stay away from these activities at all costs. These activities are also keeping you from achieving your goals. They are essentially just distracting you from doing the things that really matter. When you really get into your groove of this whole time management thing, you tend to very quickly be able to identify what you do and do not have time for. You realize how precious and valuable your time is and no longer have time for the things that are Neither Urgent or Important. Some examples include wasting time, gossiping, mindless social media scrolling, unproductive or unimportant meetings, and anything causing you to procrastinate or delay. It's important to reduce or completely avoid spending time, effort or energy on these activities. As I mentioned, when you tap into your full productivity power you will quickly be able to identify what falls into this bucket and eliminate it immediately.

It's extremely important to protect your time at all costs. By sticking to your planner, identifying which important targets will move you forward each day, and identifying what tasks you do and which productivity buckets they fall into, you will be able to protect your time so you can create more of it. You will no longer have time for the trivial things that pop up and can put your full time and energy into the things that really matter and will help you to move the ball forward. Protecting your time plays a major role in hitting your targets and goals as well as your overall success and happiness. I want you to start taking this seriously and implementing these skills in both your personal and professional life so you can be in control and live your life on your terms and on purpose.

How will time management help you hit the targets and goals you're going after?

_____
_____
_____
_____

What are the time-suckers you can identify in your life right now?

_____
_____
_____
_____

Write out a list of the goals you will achieve this month by having a clear vision of what time suckers you need to get rid of:

_____
_____
_____
_____

Key Takeaways & Notes:

6
Know your NON-Negotiables

So many of us ladies are "yes women" because we're people-pleasers. At the end of the day. we want to make sure everyone is happy and taken care of, EVEN if it means we sacrifice our own sanity. When did we decide this was OK? I don't ever remember signing up to put myself on the backburner 24/7, do you? In this chapter I am going to break down what it means to know YOUR non-negotiables. Everyone's are different, but you need to have your non-negotiables intact so you can achieve all the goals you set for yourself without becoming overwhelmed and frantic in the process, and so you can actually enjoy the things you DO say YES to!

So let's break it down. What are non-negotiables? *Non-negotiables* are the things you will *not* negotiate. They follow *your* values and principles and define not only what you will and won't accept from others, but also what you will and won't accept from yourself. They are the big-time deal-breakers! I think the biggest part of this is "what you will and won't accept from yourself." As I mentioned before, it's so easy for us as women to allow ourselves to get sucked into the YES trap. Saying yes to all the schoolroom mom activities, PTA meetings, hobbies, lessons, work obligations, and everything for everyone else but ourselves. We need to start taking back ownership of our time and days. It's up to us, and only us, to take total control of this. So I ask you, what are the things you are saying YES to now? Make a list:

YES LIST:

_____
_____
_____
_____
_____

Now make another list of all the things you are saying NO to.

NO LIST:

_____
_____
_____
_____
_____

I can almost guarantee the items you have on your YES list far exceed what you have on your no list. Why is that? I'll tell you why. It's because we feel guilty saying no to things even when it could take us away from our own happiness and growth. We feel such a need to "people please" that we will take on extra tasks, say "yes" to things we would really rather say no to, and sign ourselves up for "run-down woman of the year." Trust me, this is no badge of honor to wear. Your happiness comes from being fulfilled and living on purpose, which means is saying YES to the things you WANT to say yes to and NO to the things that do not serve you, and without feeling guilty about it.

I want you to think of the last time you committed to something you really didn't want to do. Did you feel guilty about it or were you firm on your response? Did you feel like you had to over explain yourself? The truth of the matter is this: Knowing your non-negotiables allows you to keep your stress levels down and the guilt away. So I ask you, what are YOUR non-negotiables? What are your priorities and the things you really want to say yes to? The exciting thing is how once we identify exactly what our non-negotiables and priorities are, it will be a heck of a lot easier to say NO to the things we really don't want to commit to when they come up.

Let's start with defining your priorities. What areas of life are most important to you? Work, business, self-care, community? They may all seem of high importance, but you need to know when it's time to turn off the computer and invest in some family time or get to work on that important project you have lingering. Of course, all of this is on a case-by-case basis, but once you have your priorities in order, it will be much easier for you to identify what you can say yes and no to with confidennce (key word here: *confidence*).

As a wife, mom, and entrepreneur, trust me when I tell you there is a lot going on in my world. At any moment things can change, but I am steadfast in the non-negotiables of what I have time for and what I don't. Most of my mornings look a little like this: Spending intentional time at breakfast with my son, checking in with my rock star boss babes in my FB group (*Productivity Hacks for Ambitious Women*—check it out!), then working from home, whether it be with one-on-one clients, group coaching programs, launching courses, writing a book, or publishing a new podcast episode. Every day is different, but every day I am prioritizing what needs to be done.

Being an active, engaged mama is at the very top of my priority list. I make sure no matter what I have going on in my work life, I always shut things down by the time Jakey is up from his nap, and then it's mommy/Jakey time. I just wouldn't have the same fulfillment in my work if I wasn't able to also be present as a mother, wife, and friend, as well as showing up for myself on a self-care level as well. Many of you may also be juggling and wearing many hats. I know it can be challenging at times to feel like you have to say "yes" to all the things, but the reality is YOU ARE IN CONTROL. You are in control of so much more than you give yourself credit for or than you even realize.

You are in control of your thoughts, actions, the way you respond, the way you show up, the way you fuel your body, the way you move your body, your relationships, your time, and so much more. I could go on and on.

What makes the difference between the woman who is fulfilled and living her life on purpose as opposed to the woman who is frantic, scatter-brained, and feels like she's losing control? The difference is the woman who feels fulfilled KNOWS she's in control. She knows she gets to control her environment and how she shows up. She is an active participant in life decisions. So I ask you, have you been an active participant in your life decisions or does it feel like you've been more of a bystander watching as life happens to you? It's okay to get really clear and honest with yourself right now. Now is the time to do it. Now is the time to take back control of your own ship.

I want to give you a few of my favorite tips on how to gain back control:

1. *Acknowledge you can't do everything (at once):* Trying to say yes to everything is the perfect recipe for disaster and overwhelm. Start by picking out the things you truly want to say "yes" to and honor them.
2. *Define your personal boundaries:* Defining personal boundaries isn't selfish, it's a necessity. This means you are respecting your

own personal boundaries first and foremost, and allowing anyone and everything else to show up as YOU choose.
3. *Identify your priorities*: Knowing your priorities before volunteering or responding to requests will help you gauge how much you can take on and what you are willing to take on.
4. *Don't feel like you need to be superwoman:* You can't make everyone happy, and if you try to, then the only person you will end up disappointing is yourself. Setting up non-negotiables is a way to not only set your boundaries in place, but is also a way for you to gain respect. The more respect you have for yourself in this area, the more others will too.
5. *Practice make perfect:* Practice saying no and NOT FEELING GUILTY FOR IT or feeling like you need to give a detailed explanation. If it's not your priority, that is reason enough and you don't need to feel like you have to build an entire case supporting your reasoning.

The busier our lives get the more you will want to have this plan in place. Doing this will help bring order to your life and allow you to get more of the things done you actually want to spend time and attention on, and with the people who mean the most to you versus spinning your wheels trying to think why you even said yes in the first place. It's our job as women, as leaders in our families and communities, to protect our most vital resources—time and energy. Without those, we become worn down, frustrated, and operate at levels below our true capabilities.

We are setting the tone and example for everyone around us. From our children who watch how much we take on, what we say "yes" to, and commitments we put on our plate. We are setting the tone in our businesses, with our bosses and coworkers, as to how much we are willing to take on. We set the energy in our homes with how much we take on and the stress or calm nature we bring. With every "yes" or "no" obligation you take on, *you* decide what you make time for. Make sure you are protecting your boundaries, time, and loved ones by knowing exactly where you stand on your non-negotiables. When you are clear on these boundaries, there will be no confusion on what or how much more you can add to your plate. This will help you when it comes to work, family, and personal obligations. Having this clearly defined before obligations arise will make the decision-making process even easier.

Your non-negotiables should align with your core values. How do you want to show up as a wife, mother, employee, and boss babe? What do you value most about these roles? I know for me personally, being a great wife and mother is at the top of my core values. My husband and son (soon to be sons) need to know they come first. For me, this means being the best wife and mother I can be.

Running my business and being successful in my own right is also important to me. My clients and the success of my clients are important to me. That being said, I am able to structure my work days around being the best mom *and* businesswoman I can be. I structure my days so I have time with my husband and son in the morning, my business has my attention after that until early afternoon, and then I'm in mommy/wife mode. Knowing my core values with all the hats I wear is extremely important to determine how I show up in each area. I am able to be fulfilled in each of these areas because I know what my personal core values are and what I can and should say "yes" and "no" to. Many of you get caught up in thinking you HAVE to add more to your plate. And I would question and ask you this: Does it align with your core values and non-negotiables? If it aligns with your core values, then GO FOR IT! If, in your heart, you know it doesn't, then you know what you need to do.

What does your ideal life look like to you? When you know your core values and can align them with your ideal life, then you are able to start making this process of implementing your non-negotiables much easier. Your time, how and where you show up, say so much about the choices you make and the lifestyle you choose. So choose wisely. The beauty of doing this exercise is how you get to create this exactly how YOU want and envision it. Think about where you want to spend your time, who you are spending time with, and what you show up for. You know by now how time is the most precious commodity you have, so deciding where your time goes and who it goes to should align beautifully with the life you are creating. You get to live your life to your fullest potential when you are clear on what it is you want, how you are going to make it happen, and take action.

My hope is for you to use these systems and tools to create the life you love and are destined to live—to see your true value. Know your core values, non-negotiables, and everything you bring to the table. Heck, you probably bring the whole table itself! Show up and operate with the mentality that *you* are in control of everything around you. You get to choose your own happiness, who is around you, where you spend your time, and how and where you show up! When you take responsibility for everything in your world, magic happens. Don't take these exercises lightly. As you work through them, you are working to create the life you want to live and are excited to live. Anyone can have this!

Don't doubt yourself and your amazing capabilities! My hope is for you to realize just how much control you have and how powerful you are! Without knowing your true value, it's easy to step away from our non-negotiables and let others take precious time and control away from us. Get super clear and focused TODAY (right now) on what your non-negotiables are, your personal boundaries, and what you will say YES and NO to from now on. Let's do some work on this:

List your non-negotiables:

_____
_____
_____
_____

What personal boundaries are you going to set in place?

_____
_____
_____
_____

What will you now say YES and NO to?

_____
_____
_____
_____

Key Takeaways & Notes:

7
The 3D System to Step into Success

What does stepping into success truly mean for you? This looks different for all of us, so I want you to get crystal clear on what this means for *you*. Is it more time with your family? More time on money-making moves in your business? More intentional self-care time? There is no right or wrong answer here, but it all boils down to YOU –your priorities and ow you envision success on your own terms. What do you want your life to look like? What would make you excited to get out of bed in the morning and live your life on your terms? This is how I want you to start thinking now.

In my experience as a woman who was previously burned out and on the never-ending hamster wheel of tasks, to-do lists, and everything in between, we have to be extremely intentional with our time. I remember thinking to myself before my baby was born, "How am I going to take care of our home, give my husband the attention he deserves, take care of this newborn baby, and try to find time to fit in a shower?" I remember being so overwhelmed with even the thought of trying to "do it all." I have to tell you this: Trying to do it all is a TRAP. It's a trap that will take you down a dark and scary path of stress, anxiety, and loneliness. I know what you're thinking. "I have to do it all on my own—I don't have any other choice." Wrong, girlfriend—you have 100% control of and power over your situation and circumstances. You have 100% control over how much stress, overwhelm and burden you take on. The first part in all of this is realizing you have the power!

One of my favorite methods I use at home, in my business, and to give myself that ever-so-needed "me time" we all crave is a tool I like to call the 3D System. Simply put, this 3D System stands for Do It Yourself, Delegate, or Delete. So let me walk you through this system step-by-step. When you implement this method, it allows you to take back your precious time, step out of overwhelm, and truly step into success in each area of your life. This system allows you to make decisions about what you need to act on now, pass off to someone else, or completely take off your plate. It is a game changer! It allows you to feel fulfilled because you're not spinning your wheels all day long only to end the day stressed out, exhausted, and yet asking yourself "what did I really even get done today?" Wouldn't it feel amazing to feel accomplished each day knowing you moved the ball forward in both your business and personal life? You can absolutely do this. You just need the right tools and strategies in order to implement this correctly.

The first part of the 3D system is *Do It Yourself*. These are the tasks or projects only YOU can do. These are things you wouldn't or shouldn't pass off to someone else. For example, there are tasks in my business only I can do. I create all the content I put out, I love connecting with my tribe on social media, and I am the only one in my business who can fulfill the coaching/mentorship of my clients. In my personal life, it is also extremely important to me to be a present wife and mother. There is no one else who can take my spot when it comes to spending intentional time with my family, creating memories together, or even putting my son to bed at night. When it comes to Do It Yourself, these are the tasks ONLY you can do (or would want to do). I want you to put attention on what you need to focus on right now in your personal and professional life. What are the tasks ONLY you can do? List these things and put attention on how fulfilled they make you feel. I know for me, if I was running, running, running in my business 24/7 and didn't have time for my family, I would not be fulfilled. It's important to know what only you can do, but also what brings you the most fulfillment as well as progress in your professional and personal life. I also want to note here how the things we are good at are also the things we typically enjoy doing. Evaluate if the things you decided to do yourself and keep on your plate are the best use of your time. You may enjoy doing these things, but will it move your business forward? Will this allow you to make the best use of your time? The whole idea behind this system is being able to create MORE time for yourself. In doing this, you need to get really honest with yourself and decide what you are willing to take on and do for yourself versus being smart in your business and where you put your time so you can show up 100% intentionally in each area of your life.

The second part of the 3D system is *Delegate*. If you're not someone who is used to asking for help or hiring help, this may be difficult for you in the beginning, but it will be a game-changer in your life! With all the things we have going on, there are simply not enough hours in the day to do it all ourselves. Once I released the reigns and control over things I could get help with, outsource, or delegate, I was able to show up like never before. I was able to be 100% present as a wife, mother, and woman in business. I was able to get tasks done faster, whether it was getting the groceries done, clothes washed, or tasks in my business. I realized by delegating I could essentially clone myself and get more done in the day than ever before. This truly was a game-changer in all aspects of my life.

Growing up I had (and still have) extremely hard-working parents. My mom prides herself as a woman who does it ALL. She'd work her booty off at her job during the day, come home to do homework with my brother and I at night, make dinner, clean up, get us into bed, and then slave away cleaning the house until all hours of the night, only to go to bed exhausted and wake up the next morning to do it all again. While I am extremely appreciative of what she did for us and our family, I remember seeing this at a young age and thinking there had to be a better way. There had to be a better solution to always feeling run down with no way out. I saw my mom become frustrated day in and day out, and I knew this was no way to operate or live life.

As I got older, I really took to finding solutions to help me in my own life to make things a bit easier and take items off my plate to focus on how I could get just as much done but also make progress at the same time. Whether this was as a full-time student working multiple jobs or as a wife at home who was working and running a business, and this especially kicked into high gear when I became a mother trying to run a business, home, myself, and baby at the same time. They say you truly don't appreciate your parents until you become one. Well, mom and dad, I get it. And THANK YOU!

While I think there is everything to be said and acknowledged for hard work, I also believe in working smarter, not harder. I have been able to implement this practice of delegating into every aspect of my life—at home, in my personal life, and in my business, which has allowed me to show up present, happy, fulfilled, and living out my purpose in every area of my life. I want to share with you a few of the systems and tricks I use to delegate in my life to make it much easier on myself and allow me to show up 100% in each area.

> "If you really want to grow as an entrepreneur, you need to learn to DELEGATE."
> ~ Richard Branson ~

Let me start by saying this: If someone can do something better than me or faster than me, then I'm all about delegating/outsourcing my "weaknesses" or the things I am not great at or simply would rather not do in order to create more time for myself. Think of delegating as not only saving you time but also money. Just because you are delegating/outsourcing something doesn't mean you are always spending money. This is a great way to actually buy yourself MORE TIME to focus on the money-making moves and intentional places you want to be.

Some of the systems and services I use in my own life that allow me to create more time include cleaning services—hiring someone to come into my home once a week and help me keep my area clean and organized so I can operate at maximum levels. I am also a huge fan of shopping services like Instacart, Amazon, or any other service where you can shop online and have items delivered right to your door. No longer do you have to get in the car, drive to the store, spend time picking out what you need, drive back home, and unpack. You pick your items online and it shows up on your doorstep, so all you have to do is the unpacking! Plus you're saving on time and gas, which is a total win-win in my book! Other systems and services I love for delegating are home pick-up dry cleaning services, clothing rental companies (for big events or date nights), and handyman services that come to your home or run errands for you.

In my business I am a huge fan of VAs (virtual assistants). This can be someone you hire on a per-project basis or as needed. I also love getting virtual help in my business through companies like Fiverr and Upwork. I have hired a number of VAs through these companies for help on everything from podcast editing, copywriting, and even video editing. If there is a professional job out there, you better believe there is someone who is willing to work with you to help do what needs to be done. Also, I have to add that for me to spend time shooting, editing, making a video or PowerPoint look pretty would take me HOURS! I'd much rather delegate/outsource this and have it look 100 times better than I could ever do on my own because I saved myself tons of time and money by delegating. If you're new to this, try it out and try delegating one thing at a time. This could be in your business or personal life but watch how much peace of mind, time, and stress it takes off your plate. This is going to open up so many opportunities for you and allow you "buy more time" and focus on the areas that will truly fulfill you and move you forward.

Also, I want to add that recently in one of my group coaching sessions I had one of my boss babes who is a single mom and working multiple jobs raise her hand and ask this question: "But Sandi, I don't have the extra money or help to spend on these things." Here was my response to her. YES, YOU DO! If you don't have help at home (a partner, babysitter, nanny, daycare, and so on) right now to tap into, I ask you to reconsider. Let's say you were to hire someone to come to your home and do the dishes, laundry, or even cook or organize your home for ONE HOUR. How much would this cost you? $15 or $20 MAX for an hour (depending on where you live). Now what if you used that same hour to implement taking massive action in your business implementing money-making moves? It could be onboarding a client, signing up a new customer, creating content for your business, and so on. Whatever money-making moves you know you need to do in your business that will move you forward I can GUARANTEE will bring in more money for you than the $15/$20 an hour you spent on childcare or hiring someone to come into your home for some extra help. Try it out and see how it works for you. Change your thinking.

To run a successful business you need to play to your strengths. Find out what you're good at, what moves the ball forward, and will make you the most progress in your business and focus on those! In order to gain more time in every area of your life, you need to get super-strategic about where your time is being spent. It's time to start thinking and operating like the boss babe you are. When you can get control of your time, schedule, and day, you will be able to accomplish so much more and feel incredible. This shift starts with *you*. What story are you telling yourself of what you can and can't afford and how is it holding you back? Only you can change this, but you need to see the value and the massive change this will make in your life.

Are you ready to amp up your productivity, business, and career so you can do ALL THE THINGS? Delegating is the answer here. You just need to figure out how it will work best for you. Start small, start stacking up the wins, and add on more as you feel comfortable. I can't wait to hear from you about creating more time and wins in your life once you implement this!

Lastly, we have *Delete It* in the 3D System. This is exactly what it sounds like. If, after you write out all the tasks you do in a day/week/month and you find you have those "other" items floating around that are not of high importance, do not help you bring in money, fulfill you, or move you forward, then you simply Delete It. You need to decide what is important, what deserves your attention, and what you need to simply get rid of. This could be anything from social media to getting rid of coffee dates with friends who are gossiping, or even obligations you've said "yes" to in the past that you are no longer going to put on your plate. Remember, at the end of the day *you* get to decide what stays and what goes. *You* decide how overwhelmed or fulfilled you get to feel. A few things to consider immediately taking off your plate include projects you start but will never compete, emails such as newsletter subscriptions you no longer open or care about, unproductive meetings, interruptions when you're working during peak productivity hours, clients or employees who drag their feet and hold you back from finishing projects, and tasks that can be automated, just to name a few.

The key to mastering this tool is to look for activities that aren't helping you or your business grow, along with items you can quickly drop, assign to someone else, or save for later. After you understand how your time is being spent and where the 3Ds fit into the picture, you'll be on your way to becoming a time management ninja. And, as a result, you'll get more done in your already hectic days. This system allows you to move your business forward, give you the intentional family time or "me time" you crave, and allow you to define what success means to you (on your own terms) so you can actually live it. Once you become crystal clear on the tasks you will do, delegate, and delete, you will start to create more time for yourself. This system is something you can revisit once a month, once a week, or even daily so you know exactly where your time and attention should be going.

I ask you to take some time now and plan out all of the activities that fall into these the 3D categories of Do It Yourself, Delegate, and Delete. Once you brain dump all of these items/actions, then I want you to go back and put a plan in place. If it's something you are doing yourself, give yourself a target date. If it is something you are delegating, I want you to get clear on what/who is doing it and how often. And if it is something you are deleting, decide if it is being permanently deleted or just taken off your plate for now. This 3D System will allow you to focus on the tasks and items that allow you to get strategic in your life and business so you can focus on the "money-making moves" only YOU can do. It will allow you to free up more time and energy to focus on building your brand, providing more value-added services, and increased productivity and efficiency, a;; pf which contributes to making more money and creating YOUR definition of success.

Make a list of the items/ tasks only *you* can/will DO:
_____
_____
_____
_____

Make a list of the items/tasks you will DELEGATE:
_____
_____
_____
_____

Slay Your Day

Make a list of the items/tasks you will DELETE:

_____
_____
_____
_____
_____

Key Takeaways & Notes:

8
Organizing Home and Work

Why is being organized so important when it comes to maximizing your productivity and enhancing efficiency? Let me break it down to you like this: The more unorganized, messy, and disordered your life, then the more unorganized, messy, and disordered your home, business, and daily mode of operating will be. If business or home systems are not properly organized, then tasks pile up, paperwork gets lost, and valuable time is spent on finding information or items that should be readily available. Good organizational skills can save a business and/or mama lots of time and reduce stress. I don't know about you, but as a woman who has a lot going on, the only way I can truly maximize my productivity and be on top of my game is by having an organizational system in place. I implement this everywhere from my home to my business and personal life. The more organized you are, the easier life will be!

Being organized allows you to have increased energy, feel more in control, save you time and money, reduce clutter, become better with time management, have increased efficiency, and help you set and achieve personal goals. You can see how organization is all directly correlated with time management and efficiency. But there is a difference between being effective and efficient. Being *effective* is about doing the right things, while being *efficient* is about doing things right. You want to get into the habit of not only putting your time and attention on the right things but, more importantly, you want to be putting your time and energy into doing things right. Essentially, this is the whole idea of working smarter not harder. I want to make sure the time I have is being used wisely and efficiently versus wasting time and being busy. Which would you rather be?

What does it really mean to be organized? Simply put, it means taking something that is messy, chaotic, or unordered and having it rearranged logically into a structured, coherent layout, or into specific and/or defined groups.

First, I want to dive into some organization tips you can put into place at home. These tips have helped me become more organized and efficient every day. They allow me to get more done and not turn into the stressed-out mommy monster. Both my husband and I enjoy coming to an organized house. I work from home, which makes it even more important for me to have my surroundings organized so I can work at optimal levels. Funny enough, even our son Jacob loves cleaning and organizing. I have to mention to all you mamas out there that our little ones (no matter how old) are *always watching*. From what we say, to what we do, to how we react in situations, we are helping to mold and build their reality with every step we take and move we make. If they see a clean and organized home, then they too will want to pitch in helping out around the house. Help them to build these habits now so they are used to them as they grow up and you'll be helping set them up for success in their own lives. So let's dive into some of the success hacks I have for you around home organization:

1. *Stick to a list:* Keep one on your phone or in your purse so you'll stay focused on what you need to accomplish.
2. *Resist free, unnecessary items:* Things like giveaways, hand-me-downs, and inherited items tend to just collect dust. Take items only if you'll really use them.
3. *Make your bed:* This is a great one to have kids join in on and get into the habit of doing as well. Making your bed each morning makes a huge difference in how your room looks and feels. This will be your first win of the day and helps you to keep stacking up the wins as the day goes on.
4. *Put laundry away:* Take a few minutes to put your clean, folded laundry in the drawers and closets where they belong.
5. *Bins are your best friends:* Utilize bins for everything from shoes to the kids' toys, in the bathroom and kitchen to pull the room together and make it more organized.
6. *Start a clutter collection system:* Take a few minutes to address problem areas or items

in your home. Anywhere that mess seems to accumulate is a good candidate. Identify the area and then put a system in place to organize the items in cluttered areas.
7. *Donate:* Go through your closet, kids' toys, kitchen, and so on *twice a year* and decide what items are no longer being used, If you haven't worn, played, or used an item in over twelve months, it's time to get rid of it! Set aside a bin or area in your house to designate as the donate pile. This will encourage and help everyone with their decluttering efforts.
8. *Start small:* Sometimes when you look at the entirety of a whole project it can seem overwhelming. When decluttering or organizing, start small. Start with one small area at a time. Tackle a drawer, desk, or small area and put yourself on a timer. Once the timer is up, you're done. Do this every day for those big areas you need to tackle and watch how it gets cleaned up and organized in no time!
9. *Clean out your fridge:* Take out anything in your fridge that is expired, past its prime, or smelling less than fresh. Make sure to check the main culprits like produce and leftovers first.
10. *Label, label, label:* My labeler is probably one of my favorite gadgets. I love to label anything I can! Labeling will make your life so much easier. This helps when your kids are cleaning up their areas and need some instructions/

help on putting their things away in the right spots. For kids, another great idea is to label and color code. If you have help in the house or a babysitter over who needs to know where everything is, once you have the drawers labeled it will make life a lot easier for someone else to come in and help.

> ### *Bonus Tip:*
>
> *Have a welcome station at the front door:* Wherever you most often enter your home, have this as your main "drop off station." In my home we have a basket for shoes, a bowl for keys, and a spot to put purses, diaper bags, and work bags. We are not running around to find these items at the last minute because we know exactly where these items live! This helps with showing up on time.

The list above is just a start to set you off on the right path of home organization. As I mentioned in number eight, start small if this is new to you. What I can promise you is that if you are currently living your life unorganized and do not have these systems in place yet, you are in for a wonderful surprise. As soon as you start implementing these tips you will feel more in control, less stressed, and more on top of your game! No more wasted time looking for your keys, forgetting items on your grocery list, or having piles of clutter around the home. It's time to tap into your "new normal" of organization to maximize your time and productivity! And this is just the beginning!

Let's dive in to some tips now on how you also become more productive and maximize your time at work:

1. *Clean up your desk area:* If your desk is messy, it will distract you from your work. Have a clean space to start and end each day.
2. *Don't multitask:* It sounds counterintuitive to getting more done, but the goal here isn't to get more done. The goal is to focus on quality versus quantity. We want to make sure the work you are getting done is done right.
3. *Stop procrastinating:* Procrastinating is the killer of dreams! Focus on what needs to be done and do it. Set a timer for yourself and when the timer is up, you get to be done. Get started and don't put off the hard stuff.
4. *Get the hardest thing done first*: Why is this so important to do? You want to do the hardest thing first and get it out of the way. It won't be looming over your head, and you will have the maximum amount of will power and resources available to get through what you needed to do. Everything else will seem easy after that!
5. *Use a daily planner:* If you follow me on social media or have taken any of my courses or programs, then you know I shout from the rooftops how important using a daily planner is! Schedule out what needs to be done and

the priority of when it needs to be completed. This will help to keep your day, time, and priorities on track.
6. *Use technology to your advantage:* We live in a beautiful world today where technology is possible almost instantaneously. Everything from planners to phone numbers and meetings, linking up your schedule with coworkers and even family, all these help to make sure you're on the same page and don't overbook, overlap, or even worse, forget appointments!
7. *Organize your incoming information:* Create a mail bin or have one place where all the mail comes in and you get rid of it as needed. The same goes for your email. Read then delete or take care of your emails so you only need to look at it once and then move on.
8. *Purge your office:* Declutter, empty, shred, and generally get rid of everything you don't need or want. Look around. What haven't you used in a while? Take one area at a time. If it's something that doesn't work, send it out for repair or toss it. If you haven't used it in months and can't think of when you'll actually need it, then out it goes. I want you to think about everything here—this goes for furniture, equipment, supplies, and so on. Don't forget about knick-knacks like plants (real or artificial) and decorations. If they are covered in dust and make your office looks shabby, they are fair game to get rid of!

9. *Organize your desktop:* Make sure your files, images, and documents are all in organized folders. Clear your computer desktop every day before you leave work.
10. *Establish work zones:* Decide what type of activity happens in each area of your office. You'll probably have a main work space (most likely your desk), reference area (think filing cabinet, shelves, binders), and a supply area (closet, shelves, drawers). I also have a mailing system in our home—one centralized place where all the incoming mail goes. It's a mail bin where we put all the new mail and everyone knows where to go to check it. This ensures nothing gets lots or misplaced. Having a go-to work area or work zone helps especially if you are like me and work from home. There needs to be a clear distinction between work and play zones (oh, and eating too!).

Bonus Tip:

Limit distractions: Eliminating distractions can help you stay focused and better organized at work. Don't let yourself get drawn into long social conversations when you know you need to be focused at work. Set aside certain times in the day to check your emails (instead of every five minutes) and/or return or make phone calls. If something comes up that is not on your agenda and is not an emergency, don't let it distract you from the task at hand.

Bonus Tip for Stay-at-Home Working Moms: It may be hard to limit distractions if you are working from home and do not have help/coverage from a nanny, babysitter, husband, family, and so on. Know what pockets of time you have in the day of uninterrupted time such as before the kids are up, during nap time, when they're at a playdate, or after they go to bed at night to get your most important work done. You don't want to be trying to do two very important tasks/jobs at once—watching the kids and sending out important work emails, taking phone calls, or trying to create content. Know what your optimal hours of work time are and use that time to get your most important work done!

My intention for this chapter (and the whole book) is to help all the stressed-out, overwhelmed boss babes, moms, and women of the world tap into their fullest potential. The best way to do this is by being extremely organized in all areas of life. I saw first-hand growing up how the stress of all this—running a home, working full time, and even trying to get dinner on the table—took a toll on my mom. My ultimate desire and wish is helping you to step into the best version of yourself. To step out of overwhelm, stress, and anxiety when it comes to getting all the things done by implementing systems to maximize your time and live a life of purpose. The only way you can do this is when you have control over your environment first, which means making sure you are doing everything in your power to maximize your opportunities, time, and happiness.

With a set system working more efficiently in your home and at work, you can maximize your time, get more done, and step into becoming the most fulfilled version of yourself possible. I'm excited for you to implement these tips in your own life. Where will you start? Take an inventory of the areas of your life you need to tackle first and get organized. Is getting your home organized the priority right now and where you should start, or would your office be a better place to get everything in order and organized? As I mentioned above, take one step at a time. Don't overwhelm yourself in the process, and before you know it you'll be making steps toward a more organized, stress-free home and work life. I can't wait to hear about your WINS!

What small area can you focus on now to declutter and organize?

_____
_____
_____
_____
_____

How will you commit to staying organized each day? How much time will you dedicate each day?

_____

_____

_____

_____

_____

List out the things that cause distractions for you. How can you troubleshoot to limit distractions and maximize your efficiency?

_____

_____

_____

_____

_____

Key Takeaways & Notes:

9
Take Back Control

What if you could truly be in charge of your time? What would it be like to really own your day and feel accomplished each evening knowing you not only got done what you needed to get done but are also living your life on purpose—truly being fulfilled in each area of your life? Wouldn't that feel amazing? It's not magic, it's just a little discipline and allowing yourself to practice control in your life so you can be the best version of yourself for you and everyone around you.

What does it mean to take back control of your time? Are you someone who puts things off, procrastinates, or postpones activities or tasks you need to do until the last minute? How does this make you feel? Do you operate from a place of ease or are you operating more in a frantic state? When you take back control of your time, you are able to look at the big picture. You are able to see a bird's-eye view of what you need to accomplish, what is urgent, the tasks that can wait, and what truly brings you joy. When you take back control of your time, you are able to be the captain of your own ship. You are able to take charge, step into your power, and start focusing on the things that matter most and move the ball forward faster. I want you to start thinking about the areas you can take control of. Start to think of things like your attitude, how you respond in certain situations, and what you are consuming (both mentally and the nutrients you are fueling your body with). Think about the energy you show up with, the people you surround yourself with, your work ethic, and the boundaries you set, just to name a few. Take this time to map out where you want to start. What would bring you the most progress and happiness? Start there. When you start to see how you can take back control of these aspects of your life, it makes it easier to start mapping out how and where you want to make these changes.

Doing this is vital to your success. This is something you must take ownership and control of. Incredible change happens in your life when you decide to take control of what you DO have power over. Imagine what your life will look like thirty, sixty, and ninety days from now when you start tapping into this power. By re-shifting your focus on the things you can control, you put yourself in a winning mentality. This practice will come in handy when you experience changes in life, such as when you need to navigate finding your "new normal" because of economic changes, career shifts, a move, a breakup, a new relationship, having a baby, or any other significant experience in life. Using this "what can I control" mentality allows you to see opportunities versus focusing on the struggles and hardships or feeling like a victim. The sooner you take control of your time, your surroundings, and your life, the sooner you will start seeing progress and WINS.

When you know and can focus on what you are in control of, it's a lot easier to see the opportunities right in front of you and start taking action in a positive direction.

Now that you know how important this is, let's chat about how you actually do it. In what area of your life do you feel most overwhelmed right now? What area of your life would you like to have more control over? What would having more control in this particular area bring you? I want you to start thinking about the outcome you want to experience. Do you want to feel more in control of your time? Finances? Relationships? Whatever the area may be, I want you right now to pick just one area to focus on. This could be personal, financial, or even your mindset. I want you to start thinking about all the reasons how NOT having control in this area is holding you back from being the best version of yourself. How does this make you feel? Now I want you to focus on how you would feel if you WERE in control of this area. If you were 100% accountable in this area and decided to show up 100% for YOURSELF, how would things change for you? Would you be operating differently? How would you show up? How would others view you? What would you be able to accomplish now? By focusing on the feelings and positive outcomes of being in control, you allow yourself to see what's possible. You start to see how different your life could be and how everything is truly in your hands. This is an important practice to go back to whenever you feel trapped in a victim mentality or you're navigating new waters. It puts you back into feeling the feelings and seeing the possibilities of exactly the shifts and steps you need to take to take back control, success, and happiness in your life. I'm going to quote one of my ultimate, all-time favorite movies here: "You had the power all along my dear," which is what Glenda The Good Witch said to Dorothy toward the end of *The Wizard of Oz*. You always had and will have the power. The choice to use it for good, for productivity, and for reaching your goals and dreams sooner is up to you!

I want to give you a few ways to help take back control of your time and your life you can easily implement today:

- ➢ Go to bed and wake up on a regular schedule.
- ➢ Implement a success schedule.
- ➢ Write out your planner the night before.
- ➢ Stick to a schedule.
- ➢ Cut out anything toxic - foods, friends and fake news.
- ➢ Stay away from the news.
- ➢ Cut back on caffeine and alcohol.
- ➢ Implement a daily workout routine.
- ➢ Limit your social media time.
- ➢ Read every day for at least thirty minutes.
- ➢ Invest in your mental wellbeing with positive content like podcasts and affirmations.
- ➢ Meditate daily.

- Start a daily gratitude list.
- Keep your home and workspace clean and organized.

These are just a few examples of some ways to take back control in your life and shift into a more positive and productive mindset to reach your goals sooner. Anyone can do this. It's just a matter of how dedicated you are to reaching your goals and dreams, what you're willing to put up with, and what you are committed to getting rid of to speed up your success.

There are so many benefits of taking back control in your life. When you finally take control of your life, you stop asking for permission. You get to burn the rule book and blaze your own trail. You get to make your own rules! You stop asking for other people's permission for the life you want to lead. It's no one's life but your own, and it's time you start acting like it. Taking back control allows you to stop seeking validation from outside sources. With this power, you set yourself free. Wouldn't it feel amazing to finally live life on your own terms? Why not? What's holding you back? What are you going to do now that you know how to take control of and the importance of doing this? Where is the first place you are going to start?

Imagine what taking back control means for your business, your family, your personal life, and your future. How is this going to make a huge shift in the way you operate and show up now? What are you no longer going to stand for? How are you elevating your standards now? How does this new, confident, in-control version of you feel? I can bet there are many things now you are not willing to settle for. I also am willing to bet that by raising your standards and taking back control of every area of your life means you will be able to reach your goals sooner. The fact you are now tapped into this control is such a powerful thing! You now have the ability to control exactly where your time goes, what you say yes (and no) to, and can start operating your day from a place of clear intention, which allows you to accomplish your goals sooner.

Anyone can tap into being a more accomplished version of themselves. What you do today lays the foundation for tomorrow. You can start implementing this now by finding the areas in which you struggle and what you want to tackle first. Maybe getting rid of distractions is at the top of your list so you can become more productive. Maybe setting a system in place is where you need to start, or maybe it's just focusing on one thing at a time so you can finally move the ball forward. Use the list above to implement more ways to boost your productivity. This will help you get out of your own way and finally take back control to reach your goals sooner!

In which areas of your life do you feel like you procrastinate the most? Which one do you want to take back control over now?

_____
_____
_____
_____
_____

What three action steps are you going to implement TODAY to take back control of your time and your life?

_____
_____
_____
_____
_____

How will this allow you to reach your goals sooner?

_____
_____
_____
_____
_____

Key Takeaways & Notes:

10
Claiming Your Power as a Woman Who Wants to HAVE IT ALL

This is the chapter where we tie it all together! The systems, hacks, tips, and blueprints you have been given will allow you to now step into your power and create the life YOU want to live on your own terms and as a woman who wants to "have it all!" What exactly does it mean to "have it all?" In my opinion, having it all means being fulfilled in every area. For me, showing up INTENTIONALLY every day as a wife, mom, woman in business, and putting attention on my own self-care means having it all. This will look different for everyone, and YOU are the only one who can define what "having it all" means to you.

I find so many women struggle with this idea of "perfectionism." When you try to be "perfect" (which by the way, what does that even mean or look like?), we stunt our growth and ability to get things done. We get so caught up in the minutiae and details of it all that we forget what purpose and fulfillment was driving us in the first place. We let the idea of something being "perfect" get in the way and rob us of our happiness.

I want you to establish what "HAVING IT ALL" means to you, on your own terms. Does this mean growing your business, traveling to beautiful exotic destinations, being the best wife you can be, or showing up intentionally with your kids each day? Maybe for you having it all means you investing in self-love and self-care. There is no right or wrong way to define this; it's purely what sets your soul on fire and allows you to be the most fulfilled in life. By identifying what "having it all" means to you, you start to set guidelines and boundaries in your life around what you show up for or what you will no longer put up with. This will help you more than ever identify what is important to you and how you prioritize certain tasks, people, and responsibilities. It will allow you not to feel guilty when you have to say no to something or someone. The best part about defining what "having it all" means to you is that you get to have it that much sooner. By identifying what it is you want, unapologetically, you get to tap into creating and living that life much sooner!

I want you to brainstorm now and think about all the things that set your soul on fire, the things that make you happy and that allow you to step into your power to have it all. How does this woman walk, talk, show up, and run her day? Is she bold and confident and resourceful? Is she loving and kind and caring? Right NOW you get to create how you show up from here on out. No more excuses! You have all the tools to create the day and life you've imagined on your own terms. Start implementing these tools and strategies now!

If you are unsure of HOW to step into your power, then I want to give you some tools on where to start:

- *Visualize what you want:* Visualize your goals and the life you want. Get specific about what this looks like. Who is included in this vision and how are you going to attain this?
- *Keep moving forward:* Do not allow roadblocks to be your final destination. Instead, use these blocks to pivot and find a more creative and resourceful solution. Keep moving toward your goals and don't stop until you get there.
- *Control the controllable:* Whatever is in your power to control, control it! Whatever is not in your power, accept it. Analyze what is keeping you from reaching your goals and take action on what you CAN control in the situation. The sooner you put attention on this, the sooner you will be able to move out of the circumstances you can't control and put your attention on how you can move forward toward a solution.
- Appreciate the process: Struggle and/or hardships only help set us up for success and teach us valuable lessons. Be thankful for the opportunity to learn in this process and know that struggles and hardships help make you better and stronger in the long run. If it weren't

for hard times or struggles, then we would never be growing and evolving to get better.
- *Own your ambition:* Be proud of the hard-working boss babe you are. If you're hustling in your business, then own it! If you are raising little humans, be darn proud of it (it's the toughest and most rewarding job in the world). If you're figuring out your next job, move, or side hustle, then own the fact you are in a period of growth and rebirth! Don't be afraid of declaring who you are and what you do. So many of us women downplay what we do and how we show up to serve in this world when we should be screaming our accomplishments from the rooftops. Be your own damn cheerleader and be proud of the work and goals you've accomplished! Continue to get ahead and grow by letting others know what you do, how great you are at doing it, and how you can serve them! Never doubt your own greatness and abilities.
- *Build a supportive network:* I don't know where I would be without the positive self-talk and love from my family and friends. Having a supportive, strong, and loving support system around you is key! Whether it's bouncing ideas off them, collaborating with them, or just having someone to believe in you when you forget to believe in yourself for a hot second, this cannot be overstated! If you don't have this right now, I encourage you to find the people who are

willing and able to support you, who will lift you up and show you your incredible value! If you haven't checked out the two groups I run, I highly encourage you to join us! Both are run on Facebook and have the occasional meetup or virtual meetups and weekly trainings! One is called Project In Charge- you can get more details about this at ProjectInCharge.com or you can join my *Productivity Hacks for Ambitious Women Facebook Group* as well! Both groups include POWERHOUSE women who are doing incredible things in this world, spreading positivity and are an incredible place for the women in the groups to collaborate and network at high levels! I welcome you with open arms to join one- or BOTH!!

Everything listed out here will help you to step into your power, and none of them will cost you a dime. It's straight courage, determination, having the right mindset, grit, and hard work. These are things anyone can tap into; it's just a matter of how bad you want it! What's holding you back right now? Could it be the feeling of thinking you're not good enough? Feeling sorry for yourself or inadequate? It's time to lose the victim mentality and OWN your power. You are capable, you are strong, and you are the only one who can start to make these moves in your life IF you want to HAVE IT ALL. No more excuses, distractions, or negative thinking. You attract what you focus on. So now is the time to focus on you, create the life you want, and start putting the steps into action to make it happen.

When you step into your power, it can be a pretty remarkable thing! You'll notice life doesn't magically get "easier," but it does start to flow, and opportunities do start to become more readily available to you. Wouldn't that be amazing to tap into? I want you to start taking action steps each day to tap into this power and start to identify what this looks like for you. So what will you do now? How are you going to start tapping into this power? Let's chat about what this will look like for you when you start to take action and do the work:

You're more comfortable in your own skin. You accept who you truly are—strengths, weaknesses, and everything in between. You work to your strengths and can step up and ask for help or guidance when you need it, and aren't afraid or intimidated to ask for help. You start to appreciate your body for all it is capable of and all that it does. You stop seeking validation from other people and already know YOU ARE ENOUGH!

You stand in your authenticity. This means we pull back the masks, layers, or roles we play to reveal who we really are. Authenticity means standing in your truth. The biggest and fastest way to do this is to get real and honest with yourself. Shed light on the areas where you can grow. Having the courage to show up as our authentic selves means we pave the way for others to do the same. When you are brave enough to go after your goals, dreams, and ambitions, you show other women what's possible. The easiest way to reach a bigger audience, spread your message, and have a massive impact in this world is when you show up 100% as YOU–authentically and naturally you– with all the imperfections, quirks, and qualities that make you, you! This is the fastest way to attract your tribe. With the people who resonate with you, "get" you, and who you have that automatic connection with. When you're living in true authenticity you don't hold yourself back from opportunities, or saying something "wrong" because you know YOUR people are the ones who will understand you, resonate with you, and get it. And guess what–that's all that matters!

You accept your weaknesses. Accepting your weaknesses can be tough, but it's all a part of having it all and stepping into your power. I do not pride myself on doing all the things at once. I have an amazing support system around me from my husband to parents/in-laws, childcare, delivery services, and cleaning help around the house. I take on or add support where I need it. I know what I am best at and I play to my strengths. By accepting my weaknesses, I can align myself with someone who is stronger in that area and have them on my team to ultimately make the unit, my family, and myself stronger. I want you to analyze what areas of your life you are able to identify as both strengths and weaknesses. Play to your strengths and get help or support when it comes to your weaknesses. It's okay to ask for (or hire) help! It only makes you stronger in the end. If you need to, go back and read Chapter 7 on my 3D System (Do it Yourself, Delegate, Delete). The sooner you do this the more you get done and the more fulfilled you will be. Do me a favor and if you've never done this before, try it out and see how you love it. I can guarantee it will be a game-changer in your life all around, and you won't ever want to go back!

You feel fulfilled and get to live life on PURPOSE: Something amazing happens when you finally claim and step into your power. Not only do you become more accomplished, but you also feel more fulfilled in life. I've noticed for me, the more I have going on in my businesses, at home, with my family, then the more I thrive. Living a life on purpose for me means each one of these important buckets are full. If I am lacking in the work department, then I cannot be the best mom and wife I know I can be. If I don't have the intentional time with my family I love so much, then my work suffers. You CAN have it all, just not all at the same time. It would be impossible to take on work calls and emails while trying to chase after a very active toddler. I get to live my life on purpose because of the systems I implement in all areas of my life. You get to feel fulfilled and live YOUR life on purpose when each one of the buckets important to you are full. Make a list now of each bucket or area where you need to live YOUR life on purpose to be fulfilled. Then make a list of action items that correlate with each bucket. For example, if my buckets are Family, Work, and Personal Time, how can I make sure each of those buckets get attention on a daily basis? How can you incorporate what's important to you into every day so you are being productive, moving the ball forward each day, but also being fulfilled? This is so important to dive into the more hats you wear and duties you take on.

Now it's time to step up and OWN your personal power. Once you have the vision of what you want to create and tools to step into your own power, then you can begin to identify what it looks like when you start to create this shift. It may be scary in the beginning, but I promise your life is so much better when you get to be unapologetically who you are, show up where you want, and step into your power.

You don't have to fall victim to the overworked, overstressed, and overwhelmed mentality. We so often put this burden on ourselves that just doesn't need to be there anymore. With the right tools, systems, and blueprints, you can be fulfilled in all areas! This is what I have been able to tap into for myself and countless other women who have decided that being busy, stressed, and overwhelmed was no longer the answer. There IS a better way, and it's up to you now to take this opportunity, the strategies in this book, and get to work! My heart and soul truly burst at the seams with happiness when I work with clients or they take one of my courses/programs and go from burnt out and stressed to purpose and balance. Anyone can have this. You can have this! It's time to step into the most productive and fulfilled version of yourself. You've got this! I'm here for you and I'm rooting for you! You are now ready to SLAY YOUR DAY!

What tools are you going to implement today to step into your power and highest potential?

_____
_____
_____
_____
_____

What does "Having It All" mean to you?

_____
_____
_____
_____
_____

How can you incorporate what's important to you into every day so you are being productive, moving the ball forward each day, and also being fulfilled?

_____
_____
_____
_____
_____

Key Takeaways & Notes:

11
Slay Your Day Today and Every Day

"Be the girl who decided to go for it!"

I couldn't end this book without giving you the ultimate secret to going after slaying your day today and every day. Want the secret sauce? Take all the steps, tips, and systems in this book and *get to work*. Work through each chapter. These systems have worked for countless women who went from burnt out, stressed, and overwhelmed to living a life where they are in control and fulfilled because they get to work on their dreams. Simply put, they TAKE ACTION! This book was created so you can take the tips, trainings, and blueprints covered and get to work on each layer we dive into. If you go through and only read this book, you're just doing half the work. Use this book as an opportunity to work on yourself, the systems, and processes given to you as you complete each chapter. If you come across a chapter that is a block for you, identify what the block is. Why do you find it difficult to delegate tasks in your personal or professional life? Maybe your block is getting organized and you keep finding excuses to not get your life in order. Whatever the block may be for you, identify what it is before you move on. What are the steps you will take to move past it? You will never be truly free to systemize, organize, and maximize your time if you have blocks standing in your way. Once you identify what these blocks are, then you can start to do the work to move past it. The best course of action here is doing just that—taking action! As I've mentioned in past chapters, start small, but start somewhere!

Taking action will only help move you closer each day to reaching your goals, getting control of your time, and will ultimately allow you to Slay Your Day! Add taking action to your list of non-negotiables. If you do this, not only with this book but in each area of your life, you will continue to make progress day after day.

Taking action is crucial to your success. After you take in all this information, it's important for you to take ACTION. What happens after you read a book, an article, or a blog you felt was super inspiring and could really help you move your business or life forward? Nothing happens unless you TAKE ACTION! Only through application can information really be made useful.

Actions facilitate elimination. What do I mean by this? You never know what will work for you unless you put it into action. Changing your habits and routines is an ongoing process. What you have going on today may change tomorrow, next week, a month, or even a year from now. Continuing to see what works for you and what doesn't work for you is imperative in making the necessary changes to move you forward. Making the necessary changes and paying attention to the systems and processes that do work for you will help you eliminate what is not working or helping you move forward.

Action creates habits that lead to success. Change and success is an on-going process. There is no "end game" to success. You should always be growing, evolving, and implementing new systems or strategies to ultimately make you the best version of you. When you learn these new habits and behaviors, it will take time to fully implement them. The hardest part about taking action toward change is actually getting started in the first place. The more you focus on something, the new habit or behavior that is helpful and productive, the sooner you get to reap the benefits and rewards of the change.

"Action is the foundational key to all success."
~ Pablo Picasso ~

Finally, action helps you overcome your fears. Fear can be a crippling thing. Fear is the number-one thing keeping you from reaching your goals and dreams. And you know what? Usually the fear we have is just something we have built up to be big and bad in our mind. If you can look at fear as an opportunity to grow, you can use the feeling of fear to your advantage.

There are two acronyms for fear. Forget Everything And Run or *FACE EVERYTHING AND RISE!* Which one will you choose? Every time you do something new, you face your fears and build up your confidence. You prove to yourself that not only was it not as scary as you initially thought, but you expand your comfort zone! As you continue to expand your comfort zone, little by little, you are more willing to do things that challenge you and benefit you in areas where you can grow. Nothing good ever comes from comfort zones, so use the idea and process of taking action to build that muscle to move toward getting comfortable with being uncomfortable to reach your goals! Constantly taking action creates a positive cycle that helps you create the life of your dreams.

My goal and wish for you, the boss babe who picked up this book and is ready to conquer her day, step into her power, and live life as the most fulfilled version of herself is that you take control and realize all the power you possess. You now know you control every aspect of your time, day, and life with the choices you make, how you show up, and what you are willing to accept. When you raise the bar, raise your standards, and step into your power, then you don't have time anymore for the petty little things that used to take up your time, take you away from building your empire, and creating the life of your dreams. Every step you take and decision you make is intentionally aligned with how you want to live your life on your terms.

This book encourages you to identify your goals. Come back and assess these chapters as much as needed. Revisit your non-negotiables and what you are willing to allow in your life as you continue to grow personally, financially, spiritually, and emotionally. You should always be evolving and growing. This book will allow you to tap into that power time and time again when you use it correctly. As you grow in every area of your life, decide what systems you are implementing that allow you to maximize your time and energy.

I want to leave you with this: No matter how busy, overwhelmed, stressed, and chaotic your life may seem, there is always an answer and a solution to step out of the overwhelm and into finding a solution to take back control. As we discussed in Chapter 9, control the controllable. Start to stack one small win at a time until you feel like you are making progress. Sometimes it's not about moving mountains (in business or your personal life); it's about doing what feels good and allows you to feel accomplished at the end of the day. Give yourself credit for all you do, who you show up for, and how you show up for them and know you are doing your absolute best. With all the tips, systems, and strategies implemented in your life now, you can't go wrong! You will be growing and evolving each day.

In my Facebook group, *Productivity Hacks for Ambitious Women*, I like to regularly ask the women this question: "What Went Right Today?" Whether it's a small win or a huge home run, focus on the positive and what DID go right so you can continue to stack up your wins as the days and weeks go on. The more you focus on the positive and stay solution-based, the more wins and success you will have! So I ask you now: What went right today? Give yourself a WIN right here in this moment and decide that the positive, success mindset continues to grow and flourish from here. What you focus on grows, so focus on positivity, productivity, and creating the life of your dreams. It's all here and it's possible for you. I can't wait to hear from you; to hear all about your wins, how you've amped up your productivity, implemented systems for success in every area of your life, and how you've unlocked your ultimate potential to finally SLAY YOUR DAY!

What area are you going to take ACTION on right now?

_____
_____
_____
_____
_____

How will you take action? Be specific on what you will do:

_____
_____
_____
_____
_____

Make a list of What Went Right Today:

_____
_____
_____
_____
_____

Key Takeaways & Notes:

About the Author

Sandi is a high-performance productivity coach for female entrepreneurs. She helps overwhelmed, stressed-out boss babes maximize their time, energy, and productivity to be present and intentional with the most important aspects of their lives. She helps women go from overwhelm and burnout to balance.

Sandi helps her clients achieve maximum results with her online digital courses, as well as group and one-on-one coaching. Her clients rave about how Sandi helps them turn their stressed-out, busy lives into massive productivity and being able to "balance" their time to do it all.

Sandi is also the co-founder of Project: In Charge, an online platform for ambitious women who are looking to tap into coaching, tools, and training to step into the most powerful version of themselves, gain control, and become the leader of their life.

Sandi is happily married to husband Jarrod Glandt and together they have one son, Jacob, with another son on the way. Together they reside in sunny Hollywood, Florida, where they love to enjoy days at the beach, the water park, and just enjoying time together in their backyard.

Connect with Sandi

Listen to her podcasts, Slay Your Day and Project: In Charge, on iTunes, Spotify, Google Play, or your favorite podcast app.

Follow her on Instagram @SandiGlandt.

Check out and join both of her private FB Groups: Productivity Hacks for Ambitious Women, and Project: In Charge.

Read her blog at BusinessandBody.com or ProjectInCharge.com.

Stay up to date on all the latest by signing up for her weekly emails at SandraGlandt.com.

CPSIA information can be obtained
at www.ICGtesting.com
Printed in the USA
JSHW021134070123
35908JS00002B/13